MERCEDES-BENZ BRAND PLACES

Text: Christian Marquart
Photos: Hans-Georg Esch

MERCEDES-BENZ BRAND PLACES

Architecture and Interior Design

avedition

Inhalt
Contents

Im Jahr 1997 erhielt das Architekturcenter des DaimlerChrysler-Konzerns – damals noch der Baubereich der Daimler-Benz AG – vom Vorstand des Unternehmens den Auftrag, für die Vertriebsstützpunkte der Marke Mercedes-Benz ein „Autohaus der Zukunft" zu entwickeln. Das Konzept sollte tauglich sein für eine weltweite Umsetzung.

Das Projekt stellte sich für die Mitarbeiter des Baubereichs als außerordentliche Herausforderung dar. Seine Dimensionen schienen überwältigend: Rund 6.000 Vertriebsstützpunkte auf allen Kontinenten, in allen Klimazonen und in den unterschiedlichsten Kulturen und Gesellschaften würden von diesem Vorhaben betroffen sein! Aber natürlich waren wir von diesem Auftrag und den damit verbundenen Möglichkeiten fasziniert und begeistert.

Wir wollten eine Architektur entwickeln, die weltweit um- und einsetzbar sein würde. Die dem Anspruch der Marke Mercedes-Benz entspräche. Die über viele Jahre hinweg frisch und gültig sein und nicht schon nach kurzer Zeit verbraucht und überholt aussehen würde. Die eine kontinuierliche Weiterentwicklung zuließe – und außerdem die finanziellen Möglichkeiten der Autohausbetreiber und -eigentümer nicht überforderte.

Es galt aber auch, eine Architektur zu entwickeln, welche die kulturellen Hintergründe des jeweiligen Vertriebsstandorts reflektieren und spezifische gesellschaftliche und städtebauliche Erwartungen aufnehmen und erfüllen würde. Unser ehrgeiziges Ziel: Über alle Stützpunkte hinweg einen wiedererkennbaren Marken- und Marktauftritt zu schaffen, ohne dabei Eintönigkeit und Gleichförmigkeit zuzulassen. „Vielfalt in der Einheit" wurde unser Motto. Kurzum – gefordert war das Konzept für ein gutes Stück Architektur.

Vorwort

In 1997 the Architecture Centre at the DaimlerChrysler concern – the then building centre of Daimler-Benz AG – was contracted by the board of the company to develop "a showroom for the future" for the sales points of the Mercedes-Benz brand. The concept had to be able to be used on a worldwide scale.

The project was certainly an unusual challenge for the employees of the building centre. The dimensions appeared overwhelming: Approx. 6,000 sales points on all continents, in all climatic zones and in the most varied of cultures and societies were to be affected by this plan! But we were obviously fascinated and enthusiastic about this contract and the possibilities that it brought.

We wanted to develop an architecture that could be transformed and used on a worldwide scale. Architecture that would satisfy the demands of the Mercedes-Benz brand. That would still look fresh and up-to-date for many years and not look used and outdated after only a short time. An architecture that allowed a continual development and did not exhaust the financial means of the showroom owners.

Another important aspect was to develop a piece of architecture that would reflect the cultural backgrounds of the corresponding sales locations and take on and fulfil specific societal and urban planning expectations. Our ambitious goal: a brand and brand appearance that would always be recognised without allowing for monotony and uniformity. "Variety in unity" became our motto. In short, a concept was needed for a good piece of architecture.

Preface

Einen ersten Härtetest erfuhr unsere Arbeit im Jahr 2001. Im Rahmen einer aktualisierten Vertriebsstrategie entstand das „Metropolenkonzept". Es erweitert die Palette der Autohausformate und sieht vor, in ausgewählten Großstädten Westeuropas „Mercedes-Benz Center" einzurichten. Diese Center sind die größten Stützpunkte des Vertriebsnetzes. Sie werden in den Metropolen – also etwa in Paris oder London – jeweils die gesamte Palette des PKW-Programms von Mercedes-Benz präsentieren. Ferner ist vorgesehen, in den Centern markenspezifische Ausstellungen zu zeigen und markenadäquate Events zu veranstalten.

Als Vorläufer dieses Konzepts können die Mercedes-Benz Center in Berlin und München angesehen werden. Im Kontext dieser Projekte stellte sich die Frage, ob und wie diese „Großformate" der Vertriebsstruktur in das Systemkonzept der Markenarchitektur zu integrieren seien.

Auf den ersten Blick scheinen Funktion und Größe der Mercedes-Benz Center prädestiniert dafür, im Rahmen großer Architektenwettbewerbe jeweils nach differenzierten, spektakulären Lösungen zu suchen. Auch stand der Gedanke im Raum, diese Häuser als „World Collection" der Baukunst von einer Reihe international bekannter Stararchitekten entwerfen zu lassen.

Ein wesentliches Risiko dieser Strategie war jedoch unübersehbar: Das Profil der Marke Mercedes-Benz könnte leicht mit den jeweils sehr individuellen Ausprägungen jener „Architektenmarken" in Konflikt und damit unter die Räder eines „künstlerischen" Gestaltungsimpulses geraten. So festigte sich im Hause die Position, bei der Konzeption der Architektur für die Vertriebsstützpunkte einen eigenständigen Weg einzuschlagen: eben den der Marke Mercedes-Benz.

Our work was put to its first hard test in 2001. The "Metropolis Concept" was created within the framework of the current sales strategy. It extended the spectrum of the showroom formats and aimed to set up "Mercedes-Benz Centres" in selected large towns in Western Europe. These centres are the largest bases of the sales network. They were each to present the complete spectrum of the Mercedes-Benz passenger car programme in the metropolises – such as Paris or London. A further aim was to hold brand-specific exhibitions and brand-adequate events in these centres.

The Mercedes-Benz Centres in Berlin and Munich could be seen as forerunners of this concept. In the context of this project, the question was posed whether and how to integrate these "large formats" of the sales structure into the system concept of the brand architecture.

At first sight, the functions and size of the Mercedes-Benz Centres seemed to be predestined to search for differentiated, spectacular solutions in large architectural competitions. We even toyed with the idea of having a series of internationally renowned star architects design these buildings as a "world collection" of building art.

An essential risk of this strategy was however not foreseeable: The profile of the Mercedes-Benz brand could easily end up conflicting with the individually characterised "architectural brand" and therefore falling prey to an "artistic" design impulse. Thus the position was consolidated internally to follow an individual course in the conception and design of the architecture of these sales points – that of the Mercedes-Benz brand.

Mit diesem Anspruch sind wir schließlich auch an die Entwicklung der Architektur für die Mercedes-Benz Center herangegangen. Bei diesen Projekten geht es nicht nur um Architektur, sondern auch um Städtebau: Größenordnungen von 120.000 Kubikmetern umbauten Raums sind durchaus üblich. Ziel war es, das Architekturkonzept des Projekts „Autohaus der Zukunft" in die Dimensionen der Mercedes-Benz Center zu übersetzen – in einer Weise, die den Anspruch des wiedererkennbaren Marken- und Marktauftrittes ausnahmslos für alle Vertriebsstützpunkte einlöst.

Das vorliegende Buch beschreibt den Weg, den wir seit 1997 verfolgen. Es dokumentiert die kontinuierliche Entwicklung, lässt aber auch die eine oder andere Schwäche erkennbar werden. Ein Beispiel für verbesserungsbedürftige Details ist etwa die Wortmarke „Mercedes-Benz" auf der Autohausfassade. Zunächst favorisierten wir die Verwendung von Einzelbuchstaben, später entwickelten wir aus pragmatischen und nicht zuletzt architektonischen Gründen eine Kassette mit dem Schriftzug. Auch der Einsatz von Farben wird mittlerweile zurückhaltender gehandhabt. Nicht jedes abgebildete Autohaus entspricht bis ins Einzelne den heute gültigen Standards der Systemarchitektur. Dennoch ist das charakteristische Profil und die Wiedererkennbarkeit der dokumentierten Autohäuser bemerkenswert.

Das Buch soll zeigen, wie viel Kraft, Souveränität und auch Potential für die Zukunft in einer unverwechselbaren Architektur für die Marke Mercedes-Benz liegt. Mit der Publikation verbunden ist auch ein herzlicher Dank an unsere Vertriebsorganisationen, an die Betreiber und Besitzer der Autohäuser, die uns bei der Entwicklung und Umsetzung der Architektur für Mercedes-Benz und bei der Produktion des Buchs mit viel Engagement, Geduld und Kooperationsbereitschaft unterstützt haben.

Peter Hilken
Leiter Architekturcenter DaimlerChrysler AG, Stuttgart

In the end this was the standard we aimed to achieve in the development of the architecture for the Mercedes-Benz Centres. An important aspect of these projects was not only the architecture but also the urban planning: scales of 120,000 cubic metres of built-up space are indeed the norm. The goal was to translate the architectural concept of the "showroom for the future" project into the dimensions of the Mercedes-Benz Centre – in a way that could be realised without exception in all the sales points and that satisfied the claim of being recognisable as the appearance of the brand.

This book describes the path we have been following since 1997. It documents the continual development and also shows one or two weaknesses. An example of a detail that could be improved is the word brand "Mercedes-Benz" on the showroom façade. Firstly we favoured the use of single letters; at a later date we developed a cassette with the words, from a pragmatic and of course architectural point of view. Even the use of colours in the showroom is, in the meantime, dealt with in a reserved way. Not all of the showrooms shown here correspond in every last detail to the standard of system architecture that applies today. However the characteristic profile and the recognition value of the showrooms documented in this publication is noteworthy.

The book should show how much power, sovereignty and potential for the future lies in an unchangeable piece of architecture for the Mercedes-Benz brand. Connected to this publication is a heartfelt thanks to our sales organisations, to the force behind and owners of these showrooms who have supported us with their full commitment, patience and co-operation in the development and realisation of the architecture for Mercedes-Benz and in the production of this book.

Peter Hilken

Head of the DaimlerChrysler AG Architecture Centre, Stuttgart

Von der gebauten Corporate Identity
zur Markenarchitektur
From built corporate identity
to brand architecture

Dächer lernen fliegen: Architekturdetails des Mercedes-Benz
Centers in Berlin am Salzufer

Roofs learn to fly: architectural
details of the Mercedes-Benz
Centres in Berlin at the Salzufer.

Von der gebauten Corporate Identity zur Markenarchitektur

Von der gebauten Corporate Identity zur Markenarchitektur

Seit einiger Zeit ist zu beobachten, wie Meinungsführer und Meinungsmacher des öffentlichen Lebens dem Thema Architektur erhöhte Aufmerksamkeit schenken. Das strategische Fundament des zeitgenössischen Stadtmarketings und der kommunalen Standortpolitik ist die Vermittlung urbaner Qualitäten, die wiederum wesentlich durch Architekturen manifest und damit räumlich erlebbar werden. Firmen, die auf *Corporate Identity* Wert legen, beziehen *Headquarters* und *Front Offices*, bei denen die gute Adresse und repräsentatives architektonisches Design immer wichtiger werden. Andere Unternehmen stellen als Bauherren weniger ihre korporative Selbstdarstellung als vielmehr die Profilierung ihrer Marke oder ihres Markenportfolios in den Vordergrund: Da geht es dann um eine spezielle Variante von Markenkommunikation – nämlich um Architektur für Marken. Genau das ist auch das Thema der vorliegenden Publikation.

Der gesellschaftliche Stellenwert der Architektur scheint heute – wenn auch vor einem anderen kulturellen Hintergrund – erstmals wieder annähernd so hoch wie in den ersten Jahrzehnten des vergangenen Jahrhunderts. Zwar wurde die Kontroverse um die Architektur der so genannten Postmoderne in den späten siebziger und frühen achtziger Jahren des 20. Jahrhunderts zunächst sehr temperamentvoll geführt, aber sie lief schnell ins Leere, weil Formfragen die Diskussion inhaltlicher Probleme überdeckten.

Mittlerweile sind in der täglichen Entwurfs- und Planungspraxis die semantischen, symbolischen und medialen Potentiale der Architektur mehr oder minder explizit Bestandteil funktionaler Leistungsprofile und „Lastenhefte" geworden. Weil Architektur intern wie auch in der Außenwirkung als Kommunikationsinstrument funktioniert, wird sie unter ebendiesem Aspekt in neue Verwendungszusammenhänge gestellt – etwa als Werkzeug zur Innovation von Arbeit, zur Dynamisierung sozialer, informeller und kognitiver Prozesse oder zur Prägung von Images. Mit anderen Worten: Die Architektur hat ihr Funktionsspektrum gemäß den Anforderungen der modernen Mediengesellschaft und der Wissensökonomie dramatisch erweitert.

From built corporate identity to brand architecture

For some time now we have been able to observe the fact that opinion leaders and opinion makers in public life have been paying more attention to architecture. The strategic foundation of contemporary town marketing and communal policies is the conveying of urban qualities, which are primarily manifested through architecture and can therefore be experienced "in situ". Companies that choose to place emphasis on *corporate identity* move into *headquarters* and *front offices*, where the right address and a representative architectural design become increasingly important. Other companies place less emphasis on their new buildings and on their corporate self-portrait and rather more emphasis on the presentation of their brands and brand portfolios. The latter is all about a special variant of brand communication – in particular about architecture for brands, which is the topic of this publication.

The socio-political significance of architecture today appears to be, for the first time, almost as high as during the first decades of the last century, despite its different cultural background. In the late seventies and early eighties of the 20th century there was heated controversy about the architecture of the so-called post-modern era; however, this quickly ran dry as questions of form replaced discussions about content.

In the daily drafting and planning process of today the semantic, symbolic and medial potential of architecture has more or less become an explicit component of functional service profiles and "rule books". Because architecture works internally and externally as a communications instrument, it is, in this respect, used for a variety of purposes – for example, as a tool for the innovation of work, for the acceleration of social, informal and cognitive processes or for shaping images. In other words: architecture has drastically extended its spectrum of functions according to the requirements of both the modern media society and knowledge economy.

One of the great topics in the history of architecture – "functionalism" – has thus resurfaced. However, its terms, perspectives and target groups have shifted

Ein großes Thema der Architekturgeschichte – der „Funktionalismus" – ist also wieder da. Allerdings haben sich Begriffe, Perspektiven und Adressaten deutlich verschoben. Was in den zwanziger Jahren in Deutschland im Einflussbereich der Bauhaus-Lehren entworfen und gebaut wurde, interpretiert die Kulturgeschichte heute gewissermaßen als verräumlichte Ausdrucksform der Weimarer Republik, obwohl (oder gerade weil) damals selbst die Stars der Architektur-Avantgarde im Wesentlichen nur Projekte im Wohnungs- und Siedlungsbau realisieren konnten und an Aufträge für repräsentative „Staatsarchitektur" gar nicht zu denken war. Heute ist es vor allem die Wirtschaft, sind es Unternehmen und *Brands,* welche das „Gesicht" der zeitgenössischen Architektur in seinen großen Zügen prägen, weiterentwickeln und, ja: globalisieren.

Wirtschaftsarchitektur als kulturelles Leitmedium einer globalisierten Welt: Klingt das nicht allzu sehr nach Diskriminierung etwa bedeutender Kulturbauten, die in jüngerer Zeit in Europa, Amerika und Japan entstanden sind und weltweit Aufsehen und Bewunderung erregten? Nüchtern betrachtet sind jene berühmt gewordenen Museen, Theater und Opernhäuser durchweg famose Einzelleistungen eines ziemlich kleinen, dafür sehr internationalen Kreises von Baukünstlern. Als *Flying Circus* ständig zwischen den Kontinenten unterwegs, können die Stars der Architektenszene jedoch weder an den Orten ihres Wirkens noch anderswo tatsächlich „Schule machen". Denn die konkreten Realisierungsbedingungen ihrer Projekte und auch ihre Architektursprachen sind jeweils viel zu spezifisch bzw. individuell, um allgemeine Standards setzen, einen Stil oder auch nur eine gepflegte Mode prägen zu können.

Nicht zufällig befasst sich der deutsche Rat für Formgebung (German Design Council) – ein Institut, das sich in der Vergangenheit vor allem und fast ausschließlich um die Förderung des Produkt- und Kommunikationsdesigns verdient gemacht hat – neuerdings mit dem Verhältnis von Baukultur und Wirtschaftskultur, genauer: mit dem Zusammenhang von Architektur und Markenkommunikation. Im Begleitheft eines (ersten) vom Rat für Formgebung veranstalteten Fachkongresses zum Themenkomplex

significantly. What was designed and constructed in Germany in the twenties under the influence of the Bauhaus is, to a certain extent, interpreted by today's cultural historians as a spatial expression of the Weimar Republic. This is despite the fact (or perhaps because of the fact) that at the time even the stars of the architectural avant-garde could basically only realise projects in apartment and housing schemes and were not even considered for contracts involving representative "state architecture". Today it is primarily the commercial sector, companies and *brands*, which shape, develop and indeed globalise the face of contemporary architecture.

Commercial architecture as the primary cultural medium of a globalised world: does this not sound too much like discrimination of significant cultural buildings which were recently constructed in Europe, America and Japan and which created a sensation? Plainly speaking, all of these famous museums, theatres and opera houses are splendid individual pieces of work by a relatively small but very international circle of architectural artists. However, as a *Flying Circus* continually travelling between continents, the stars of this architectural scene cannot really "create a following", neither at their place of work nor anywhere else. The actual building conditions for their projects as well as their architectural expressions are too specific or individual to be able to set a general standard, create a style or even shape a fashion.

The German Design Council, an institute which in the past almost exclusively concerned itself with the promotion of product and communication design, has now deliberately begun to deal with the relationship between building culture and commercial culture, or more precisely with the connection between architecture and brand communication. In the supplementary booklet for the (first) German Design Council's Trade Congress on Corporate Architecture, under the title "Architecture for Brands" (2002), the introduction reads as follows: "Over the last few years architecture has definitely become a leading discipline amongst the design disciplines. The same can be applied to the brand as a model of the globalised economy. The creation, development and nurturing of a strong brand is at the centre of all corporate strategies.

**Wenn die Fassade zum
Schaufenster wird: Mercedes-
Benz Center in München**

When the façade becomes a
shop window: the Mercedes-
Benz Centre in Munich.

**Mercedes-Benz Center Berlin:
Jedes Fassadenelement ist
sorgfältig gestaltet.**

Mercedes-Benz Centre Berlin:
every element of the façade
has been carefully designed.

Von der gebauten Corporate Identity zur Markenarchitektur

Corporate Architecture mit dem Titel „Architektur für Marken" (2002) heißt es einleitend: „Die Architektur hat sich in den vergangenen Jahren eindeutig zur Leitdisziplin unter den Gestaltungsdisziplinen entwickelt. Gleiches kann für die Marke als Leitbild der globalisierten Wirtschaft gelten. Eine starke Marke zu schaffen, zu entwickeln, zu pflegen, steht im Zentrum jeder Unternehmensstrategie. Die Verbindung zwischen Marke und Architektur ist Kommunikation ..."

Welches Potential an Wirtschafts-, Alltags- und Hochkultur der Rat für Formgebung in der Amalgamierung von unternehmerischer „Architekturpolitik" und Markenstrategie sieht, erhellt in derselben Textquelle (*Anlage 1 spezial*, Hrsg. Rat für Formgebung, 13/2002, S. 13) ein mutiger Verweis auf Analogien des Konzepts der Marke und der traditionsschweren Idee des Gesamtkunstwerks: „Das Konzept der Marke ist mit dem Konzept Gesamtkunstwerk insofern vergleichbar, als es für seine erfolgreiche Umsetzung den Anspruch auf Ganzheitlichkeit erheben muss. Die raumbildende Disziplin Architektur ist in ihrer Vielschichtigkeit und kommunikativen Überlegenheit gegenüber den anderen Gestaltungsdisziplinen nicht nur bloßer Bestandteil der Markeninszenierung. Die Bedeutung der Architektur als Zeichen, das nicht virtuell, sondern verortbar ist, steigt angesichts der Entkörperung unserer Wirtschaft in der postulierten Dienstleistungs- und Wissensgesellschaft. Die unsere Zeit prägenden Phänomene Marke und Architektur werden sich in Zukunft noch stärker aufeinander einlassen."

Die vorliegende Publikation vermeidet es, Strategien der Markenbildung, -prägung und -führung in die Nähe des Phänomens „Gesamtkunstwerk" zu bringen. Aus einem einfachen Grund: Die vom Komponisten Richard Wagner im 19. Jahrhundert propagierte Idee hat zwar Wirkung gezeigt, aber nie richtig funktioniert. Das System der Markenökonomie war dagegen sehr erfolgreich, wurde aber – sieht man von der feinen, kleinen Kaste der Marketingstrategen und „Markengurus" einmal ab – in seinen Mechanismen weder von Verbrauchern noch von Produktherstellern wirklich verstanden. Die ganz großen, traditionsreichsten, weltweit in den Märkten präsenten Marken sind in ihrer fast mythischen Qualität weniger gemacht als vielmehr gewachsen.

The connection between brand and architecture is communication ..."

In the same text (*Anlage 1 spezial*, published by the Design Council, 13/2002, p.13), the Design Council refers, quite boldly, to analogies between the concept of brands and the traditional idea of a complete work of art ("Gesamtkunstwerk"). It therefore highlights the potential of an amalgamation of the corporate "architectural policy" and marketing strategy for our commercial, street and high culture. "The concept of the brand is comparable to the concept of the complete work of art in as much as it needs to meet a holistic standard to be realised successfully. The spatial discipline of architecture is, due to its complexity and superiority in comparison to other design disciplines, not only another part of the marketing process. The importance of architecture as a symbol, which is not virtual but localised, is increasing due to the incorporeal nature of the economy in our postulated service and knowledge society. The phenomena of brands and architecture, which is so characteristic of our time, will become increasingly interlinked in the future".

The following publication does not forge a connection between strategies for the design, shape or management of brands with the idea of a complete work of art ("Gesamtkunstwerk"). The reason behind this is a simple one: the idea propagated by the composer Richard Wagner in the 19th century had an effect but it never really worked. The system of the brand economy was, on the other hand, very successful. It was, however, never completely understood by the consumers nor the producers – apart from a sophisticated small caste of marketing strategists and so-called "brand gurus". The very large, traditional brands, which are available around the globe and have an almost mythical quality, have not been created but have rather grown.

Nevertheless this publication also supports the idea that brand strategies and policies can only be truly successful on the basis of a consistent and very detailed concept. On the whole, brand messages can only be effectively communicated if their content is synaesthetic and if their language is emotional as well as "charged" with a value system which harmonises

Gleichwohl folgt auch dieses Buch dem Gedanken, dass Markenstrategie und -politik nur auf der Grundlage eines ganzheitlichen, sehr umfassenden Konzepts erfolgreich sein kann. Markenbotschaften können wirksam nur kommuniziert werden, wenn ihre Inhalte synästhetisch aufbereitet, emotional formuliert und mit einem Wertesystem „aufgeladen" werden, das mit den kulturellen, ja sogar den spirituellen Bedürfnissen der Konsumenten harmoniert.

Entsprechend vielfältig sind die Themen dieses Buchs. Am Beginn steht eine Folge von Kapiteln, in denen kurz die Rolle von Marken im Wirtschaftsgeschehen, das Funktionieren von „Markenwelten" und ihre Umsetzung in systemische Markenarchitekturen beschrieben werden – natürlich vor dem Hintergrund der Marke Mercedes-Benz und den traditionellen wie künftigen Strukturen der Bauaufgabe „Autohaus".

In den weiteren Abschnitten des allgemeineren Teils geht es um die Prägung der Marke Mercedes-Benz und um das Markenerlebnis in den „Brand Galleries" der Zukunft, um Farb- und Lichtdesign in den Autohäusern von Mercedes-Benz, um den Einsatz von Medien für Vertrieb und Marke und schließlich um den Zusammenhang von Event-Marketing und Architektur.

Die Darstellung der Mercedes-Benz Center in Berlin und München, deren Architektur noch nicht dem Systemgedanken folgt, bildet gewissermaßen das Scharnier, das die einleitenden und allgemeineren Kapitel mit den konkreten Beschreibungen der nach einheitlichen Form- und Konstruktionsprinzipien gestalteten Mercedes-Benz Autohäuser in aller Welt verbindet. Hier wird gezeigt, welche formalen, konstruktiven und stilbildenden Prinzipien dafür sorgen, dass die jüngere Retail-Architektur von Mercedes-Benz über alle Kontinente hinweg wiedererkennbar bleibt und folglich die Identität der Marke stützt.

with the cultural or even spiritual requirements of the consumers.

Thus this book contains a variety of topics. At the beginning you will find a series of chapters which briefly describe the role of brands in the economy, the functioning of "brand worlds" and their transformation into systematic brand architecture. Naturally the chapters are written against the background of the Mercedes-Benz brand as well as the traditional and future structures of the building of "car dealerships".

Further sections in the general part of the book are dedicated to the following: the shaping of the Mercedes-Benz brand and the brand experience in the "Brand Galleries" of the future, the colour and light design in the Mercedes-Benz showrooms, the use of media in sales and brands and, finally, the connection between event marketing and architecture.

The architecture of the Mercedes-Benz Centres in Berlin and Munich does not yet follow the systematic design idea. To some extent, the portrayal of these centres is used as a hinge connecting the introductory and general chapters with the concrete descriptions of the Mercedes-Benz car dealerships around the whole world, which were designed according to the unified design and construction principles. It successfully demonstrates which design, construction and stylistic principles ensure that the more recent retail architecture by Mercedes-Benz remains recognisable in all continents and consequently supports the identity of the brand.

Eine Fülle horizontaler und
vertikaler Perspektiven und
Sichtachsen hält die Neugier
wach und das Publikum
in Bewegung: Innenraum
des Mercedes-Benz Centers
in Berlin

A host of horizontal and
vertical perspectives
and angles holds interest and
the public in motion: interior
rooms of the Mercedes-Benz
Centre in Berlin.

Was sind Marken und wie funktionieren sie?
What are brands and how do they work?

Wie Bücher im Regal: Im
Setzkasten sind die Modell-
reihen der Marke präsent.

Like books on a shelf: All
the brand's series of models
are present in the case
compartments.

Was sind Marken und wie funktionieren sie?

Was sind Marken und wie funktionieren sie?

In der Ökonomie der Markenwelten geht es nicht mehr allein um Produkte und Produkteigenschaften, sondern um komplex aufgebaute Wertsysteme, die als *Brands* untereinander in einen Wettbewerb um Aufmerksamkeit und Wertschätzung treten. *Brands* entwickeln ein erstaunliches Eigenleben, sie können und sollen sich gewissermaßen zu individuellen Markenpersönlichkeiten entfalten und weiterentwickeln. Reale Produkte oder Dienstleistungen sind in diese virtuellen Konstrukte eingebettet wie ein Skelett in einen Organismus.

Der Kosmos der Markenwelten, die zum Teil noch miteinander durch Strategien des Co- und Cross-Branding verknüpft werden, steht durch den Rekordbestseller *No Logo* der Kanadierin Naomi Klein seit einiger Zeit im Schnittpunkt einer verschärft geführten öffentlichen Diskussion. Die von Naomi Kleins Argumenten geprägte Kritik an der Markenökonomie geht zwar am Thema und an der Marke Mercedes-Benz vorbei, denn *No Logo* attackierte primär die Wertschöpfungslogik jener Konsumgütermarken, deren Produkte zu minimalen Kosten und oft unter fragwürdigen Bedingungen („Sweat Shops") in unterentwickelten Ländern hergestellt, auf den Märkten der Industrienationen aber zu Maximalpreisen verkauft werden. Dennoch soll hier kurz auf einen Generalverdacht der Markenkritiker eingegangen werden, der verkürzt behauptet: Die strategisch betriebene Pflege von Markenmythen betreibe erstens die intellektuelle Entmündigung des Konsumenten; zweitens sei es ein flagranter Missbrauch von Kulturtechniken, wenn kulturelle und im Extrem sogar quasi-religiöse Rituale in den Dienst der Marken und damit in den Dienst kommerzieller Vertrauensproduktion gestellt würden.

Wohl ist richtig: Marken bieten dem Publikum Orientierung in unübersichtlichen Märkten. Und weil Marken im Erfolgsfall tatsächlich Vertrauen erzeugen und Begehrlichkeiten wecken, lässt sich auch schwerlich abstreiten, dass in diesem Wechselspiel kulturelle Verhaltensmuster und -mechanismen wirksam werden. Vertrauen ist allerdings nicht allein ein Begriff aus der Vorstellungswelt der Moral bzw. der traditionellen Ethik. Im Kontext der Gesellschaftswissenschaften und insbesondere in der Theorie sozialer Systeme gilt

What are brands and how do they work?

In the economy of brand worlds we are not only dealing with products and the qualities of product any more, we are dealing with complexly developed value systems – *brands* which compete with each other for the attention of and evaluation by the public. *Brands* develop their own life to an astounding extent, and to a certain degree they can and should evolve into individual brand personalities and develop further. Real products or services are embedded in these virtual constructs like a skeleton in an organism.

The cosmos of the brand worlds, which are still partly connected to one another by the strategies of co- and cross-branding, have been subject to heated public discussion for some time due to the Canadian author Naomi Klein's record bestseller "No Logo". The criticism of the brand economy based on Naomi Klein's critique do not affect this topic and the Mercedes-Benz brand as "No Logo" primarily attacks the logics of net production of all consumer goods markets, whose products are manufactured at minimal costs and often under questionable circumstances ("sweatshops") in underdeveloped countries and then sold at maximum prices on the markets of the industrial nations. However we should briefly go into the general suspicion presented by the brand critic at this point, who in short claims: The strategically practiced maintenance of brand myths firstly instigates the intellectual incapacitation of consumers: Secondly it is a flagrant abuse of culture techniques, if cultural or even quasi-religious rituals were used to serve brands and thereby serve the commercial creation of trust.

It is absolutely correct: Brands offer the public an orientation in unclear markets. And as brands, in successful cases, actually do create trust and awaken desirability, it is hard to dispute that in this interplay cultural behaviour patterns and mechanisms have an effect. Trust is however not merely a term from the imaginative world of moral and traditional ethics. In the context of social sciences and, in particular, in the theory of social systems the building up of trust is considered more or less to be a consciously and rationally applied instrument which only thus makes it possible for the individual, societal groups and state

Vertrauensbildung als ein mehr oder minder bewusst und rational eingesetztes Instrument, das es Individuen, gesellschaftlichen Gruppen und staatlichen Organisationen überhaupt erst möglich macht, in einer unübersichtlichen Welt mit offener Zukunft handlungsfähig zu bleiben.

In seiner 1968 veröffentlichten Studie „Vertrauen" analysierte der Soziologe Niklas Luhmann in kühler Brillanz die Voraussetzungen und Prozesse gesellschaftlicher Vertrauensproduktion. Das kleine Werk böte Markenexperten hinreichend Material, um einerseits ihre Strategien zu reflektieren bzw. zu perfektionieren – und andererseits den Kritikern der Markenkultur Paroli zu bieten; seltsamerweise wird es aber in dieser Hinsicht kaum genutzt.

Luhmanns Grundüberlegung: Die vor allem technisch erzeugte Komplexität unserer Umwelt nimmt ständig zu und erfordert mehr und mehr die Inanspruchnahme der Ressource Vertrauen, weil das Geschehen von niemandem mehr durch individuelle Sachbeherrschung zu kontrollieren ist. Vertrauen und Misstrauen seien, so Luhmann, „symbolisch vermittelte, generalisierte Haltungen, die (...) durch subjektive Prozesse der vereinfachenden Erlebnisverarbeitung gesteuert werden."

Analog zum „Lernen des Lernens" ist nach Luhmann das „Vertrauen in Vertrauen" bei der Bewältigung des Alltags besonders effizient, speziell dann, wenn in dieser Sache eine gesellschaftliche Übereinkunft erzielt werden kann. Auf dieser Ebene wird das Vertrauen dann zur Konvention, zum „Systemvertrauen" – also zu einem Zivilisationsprodukt. Und schon sind wir bei der Orientierungsfunktion von Marken und ihrer kulturellen Grundlage.

Luhmanns Analyse des Phänomens Vertrauen als Disposition zu durchaus rationalem Verhalten in unübersichtlichen Verhältnissen (die sich umstandslos als strategisches Marken-Kompendium lesen lässt) übersieht natürlich nicht die emotionale Vielschichtigkeit des Themas. Ohne eine stabile Gefühlsbeziehung zu *individuellen* Objekten oder Menschen entsteht keine Vertrauensbereitschaft und ohne jene kein Vertrauen: „Gefühle schließen prinzipiell alle Aspekte ihres Gegenstandes ein. (...) Sie schließen alle anderen

organisations to remain capable of acting in an unclear world with an uncertain future.

The sociologist Niklas Luhmann analysed the conditions and processes of societal trust production. This study "Vertrauen" (Trust), published in 1968, was written with a cool brilliance. This small piece of work offered brand experts sufficient material to, on the one hand, reflect and perfect their strategy, and on the other hand, to stand up to critics of the brand culture; strangely it is hardly used in this respect.

Luhmann's basic ideas: it is mainly the technically produced complexities of our environment that are continually increasing, demanding more and more claim of the resource Trust, because nobody can control events through individual expertise any more. Trust and mistrust are, according to Luhmann, "general attitudes which are conveyed through symbols and controlled by the subjective process of simplified experiences".

Further Luhmann states: Analogue to the "learning of learning", the "trust in trust" is particularly efficient in coping with everyday life; especially when a societal agreement can be made in this matter. On this level, trust then becomes a convention, becomes a "trust of the system" – that is a product of civilisation. And here we arrive at the orientation functions of brands and their cultural basis.

Luhmann's analysis of the phenomenon of trust as a disposition to behave in a certainly rational manner in unclear circumstances (which without further ado allow themselves to be read as a strategic brand compendium) obviously does not oversee the emotional complexity of this subject. Without a stable relationship feeling-wise to *individual* objects or people, no readiness to trust is created, and without this there is no trust: "Principally feelings include all aspects of their objects (...). They exclude all other objects or comparatively put them aside, even if, in certain cases, they are equal or better. With this they define... an insensitivity for other things, which remains astounding to all others with the same experience if they do not share the same experience."

Selbstähnlichkeit als Prinzip: eines der neuen Autohaus-Formate in Korinth / Griechenland

Self-similarity as a principle: one of the new showroom formats in Corinth / Greece

Noch im Schattenwurf bewahrt
die neue Systemarchitektur
der Mercedes-Benz Autohäuser
ihre Charakteristik.

The new system architecture of
the Mercedes-Benz showroom
even retains its character when
seen as a shadow.

Was sind Marken und wie funktionieren sie?

Gegenstände aus oder stellen sie doch vergleichsweise zurück, selbst wenn sie in einzelnen Hinsichten gleiche oder bessere Leistungen aufweisen. Damit fixieren sie ... eine Unempfindlichkeit für andere Dinge, die für alle Miterlebenden erstaunlich bleibt, wenn sie das Gefühl nicht teilen."

Stellt man in Anlehnung an Luhmann in Rechnung, dass die vertrauensvolle Orientierung der Verbraucher an Marken, Markenwerten und Markenbotschaften nicht nur ein gehöriges Maß an ziviler Verhaltensrationalität aufweist, sondern auch Ausdruck neu formulierter gesellschaftlicher Konventionen ist, welche die mittlerweile dispensierten traditionellen Codices (bildungs-)bürgerlichen Verhaltens ersetzen mussten, lässt sich die kulturelle Dimension der Markenökonomie kaum noch leugnen. Auch die Nähe der Markenmythen zur Sphäre des Spirituellen und die daran vollzogenen „liturgischen" Kaufhandlungen wirken nicht sonderlich bizarr, wenn man zur Kenntnis nimmt, dass Kultur im 20. Jahrhundert ohne nennenswerten Widerstand der Gesellschaft zur „Zivilreligion" werden konnte.

Ein Zwischenergebnis der vorangestellten Betrachtungen könnte deshalb lauten: Marken dienen der Kulturierung der Märkte, der Kultivierung der Technik und nicht zuletzt der Ästhetisierung des Alltags. Marken unterstützen die Ausdrucks- und Distinktionsfähigkeit der Individuen.

Das alles kann aber nur funktionieren, wenn Marken ihrerseits den Ansprüchen genügen, die ihr kultureller „Überbau" ihnen abverlangt. Ein Bonmot des Staatsrechtlers Carl Schmitt aus den frühen dreißiger Jahren lautet: „Der Weg vom Metaphysischen und Moralischen zum Ökonomischen geht über die Ästhetik." Im Kontext unseres Markenthemas wäre dieser Satz am besten rückwärts zu lesen und zu interpretieren: Ohne ein ästhetisches, ohne ein kulturell verankertes und damit auch emotional aufgeladenes Konzept sind Marken nicht wirksam zu gestalten und zu inszenieren – und sie erreichen nie den Status eines Mythos.

Marken sind vieles zugleich: ein Bündel von Metaphern, Bedeutungsraum, ein System symbolischer Verweise und Abgrenzungen, eine mehrfach codierte

The cultural dimension of the brand economy can hardly be denied if you take the following assumptions into account, according to Luhmann: The consumers' trusting orientation towards brands, brand values and brand messages demonstrates a sizable degree of civil and rational behaviour. In addition, it is an expression of a new social convention which had to replace the – now discarded – traditional behaviour/al codes of the educated classes. The close links of the brand myths to the spiritual sphere and the related "liturgical" acts of buying/purchasing activities are not particularly bizarre when you think that in the 20th century culture has managed to become a "civil religion" without any significant resistance from society.

An interim result of the preceding observations could therefore read: Brands serve the culturing of markets, culturing of technologies and, last but not least, the "aestheticising" of everyday life. Brands support individuals in the ability of expression and distinction.

But all this can only work if the brands themselves satisfy the requirements on their own side, which are demanded from them and defined by their cultural "superstructure". A bon mot from the national lawyer Carl Schmitt from the early thirties states: "The path leading from the Metaphysical and Moral to the Economic goes over Aesthetics." In the context of our brand subject, this sentence is best read and interpreted backwards: Without an aesthetical, culturally anchored, and therefore also emotionally charged concept, brands cannot be designed and stage-managed effectively – never achieving the status of a myth.

Brands are a lot of things at the same time: a bundle of metaphors, a space full of meanings, a system of symbolic references and delimitations; a multiply-coded message with considerable leeway for associations, desires, dreams and expectations (which can be fulfilled); a diversely usable means of expression and distinction; a promise of stability and value and much more besides.

Products can be touched but brands cannot. The latter have to be communicated and made "experienceable", one the one hand in the products themselves and on the other hand in suitable surroundings. These

Botschaft mit großen Spielräumen für Assoziationen, Wünsche, Träume und (erfüllbare) Erwartungen, ein vielfältig einsetzbares Ausdrucks- und Unterscheidungsmittel, ein Versprechen von Stabilität und Wertigkeit und vieles andere mehr.

Produkte sind anfassbar, Marken aber nicht. Letztere müssen einerseits am Produkt selbst, andererseits aber in einem geeigneten Umfeld kommuniziert und „erlebbar" gemacht werden. Dieses Umfeld hat medialen und räumlichen Charakter. Es ist vielschichtig, aber in sich logisch und konsistent und unter synästhetischen Aspekten zu konfigurieren. Ein Gesamtkunstwerk? Der Umgang und das Geschäft mit Marken ist eher eine Sache von Gesamtkunsthandwerkern: Produkt-, Medien- und Event-Designern, Kommunikationsexperten, Szenografen und last but not least Architekten. Sie alle stehen unter dem strengen Diktat der Marke. Das, was sie ist, und alles, was sie werden soll, bestimmt und prägt alle kommunikativen und gestalterischen Prozesse.

Keine einfache Aufgabe. Denn es fällt Marketing- und Brand-Managern nicht immer leicht, die gewollt vielschichtige bzw. mehrdimensionale Ausprägung von Markenbotschaften und -merkmalen so präzise zu fassen, dass sie als Handreichungen für Gestalter dienlich sein können. Für dieses Dilemma hat der Kulturhistoriker Jacob Burckhardt schon im vorletzten Jahrhundert die richtigen Worte gefunden: Kultur, meinte er, sei Nervensache.

surroundings have a medial and spatial character; it is complex but with an inner logic, is consistent and can be configured under synaesthetic aspects. A synthesis of the arts? The dealing with and business with brands is really something for art craftsmen: product and media designers, event specialists, communication experts, scenographers and, last but not least, architects. All of them are strictly dictated by the brand. That which it is, and everything it is supposed to be, determines and characterises all the communicative and design processes.

Not an easy task. It is not always easy for marketing and brand managers to express precisely the desired complex and multi-dimensional form of brand messages and characteristics, so that they can serve as a helping hand to designers. The cultural historian Jakob Burckhardt found the correct words for this very dilemma in the century before last: Culture, he said, is a question of nerves.

Kommunikation rund um
die Uhr: Markenarchitektur
muss zu jeder Tageszeit
„funktionieren".

Communication around the
clock: Brand architecture has
to "work" at all times.

Die Funktionen des Mercedes-Benz Autohauses
Functions of the Mercedes-Benz car dealerships

Auch der Werkstattbetrieb erzählt von Markenhaltung und -werten.

Even the garages talk of the brand and its values.

Die Funktionen des Mercedes-Benz Autohauses

Functions of the Mercedes-Benz car dealerships

Eine Architekturgeschichte des Autohauses steht noch aus. Beginnen könnte sie in unterschiedlichen Varianten: etwa als Geschichte der Manufakturen, die ihre Produkte zunächst noch direkt vom Fabrikhof weg verkauften; als Chronik des Aufbaus von überregionalen oder gar transkontinentalen Vertriebswegen und Handelsvertretungen; oder als Handwerkerlegende, welche die Geschichte jener Autoschlossereien zu erzählen hätte, die mit Karosseriebau, Reparaturen und Service-Angeboten ganz klein anfingen, um schließlich zu großen Markenhäusern mit üppigem Leistungsportfolio heranzuwachsen.

In der Absicht, seinen Motoren und Fahrzeugen einen größeren Markt und mehr Popularität zu verschaffen, rief Gottlieb Daimler 1896 in Stuttgart das erste Taxi-Unternehmen der Welt ins Leben – die „Daimler Motorwagen-Kutscherei". In Amerika hatte er sich schon zuvor mit William Steinway verbunden, dem Inhaber der berühmten Piano-Fabrik Steinway & Sons in New York. Steinway erwarb von Daimler Lizenzen und gründete an der Bowery Bay die „Daimler Motor Company" sowie ein Verkaufsbüro in Manhattan in der 14. Straße.

Pianos plus Pferdestärken? Aus heutiger Sicht wirkt diese Partnerschaft wie eine frühe Cross-Branding-Strategie. Tatsächlich kamen in den Anfangsjahren des Automobilismus die Markenwerte eines Fahrzeugs (sofern schon entwickelt) ganz und ausschließlich im Produkt selbst zum Ausdruck. Dessen primäres Umfeld – die Sphäre der Fabrikation, des Fahrzeug- und Ersatzteilevertriebs und der Werkstätten – bedurfte noch keiner speziellen Inszenierung. Das „Autohaus" in allen seinen Varianten, ob groß oder klein, war deshalb über viele Jahrzehnte rein funktional, das heißt allein gemäß betrieblicher und betriebswirtschaftlicher Erfordernisse organisiert. Die Marke und ihre Botschaften spielten bei der räumlich-architektonischen Planung keine oder nur eine sehr untergeordnete Rolle.

Erst in den letzten zehn Jahren nahm die Idee, markengebundene Handelshäuser weltweit innen wie außen nach einheitlichen Kriterien zu gestalten und ihnen eine *Brand Identity* aufzuprägen, auch in

Functions of the Mercedes-Benz car dealerships

An architectural history of car dealerships is still owed here. It could begin with several different variations: perhaps as the history of manufacturers who originally used to sell their products directly from the factory yard; as a chronicle of the establishment of nationwide or even transcontinental sales paths and commercial travellers; or as a legend of craftsmen, the history of which could have been told by any "body shops" who began on a very small scale with bodywork construction, repairs and offers of service and who later grew into large brand houses with luxurious service portfolios.

With the intention of creating a larger market and increased popularity for his motors and vehicles, Gottlieb Daimler founded the first taxi company in the world in Stuttgart in 1896 – The "Daimler Motor-Wagen-Kutscherei". At the time, he was already associated with William Steinway in America, the owner of the famous piano factory Steinway & Sons in New York. Steinway acquired licences from Daimler and founded the "Daimler Motor Company" at Bowery Bay as well as a sales office in 14th Street in Manhattan.

Pianos plus horsepower? Today this partnership would be seen as an early cross-branding strategy. In actual fact in the early years of automobiles, the brand value of a vehicle (as much as it had been developed) was expressed totally and singularly in the product itself. Its immediate environment, that is, the manufacturing space, the sales and replacement parts areas, did not need a particular staging as yet. The car dealership in all its variations, whether large or small, was purely functional for many decades, meaning it was only organised from an operational and business management point of view. As far as the spatial-architectural planning was concerned, the brand and its messages did not play a role or, if they did, it was a secondary one.

It was only in the last ten years that the idea also gradually took form in the car industry of creating branded commercial dealerships designed on the inside as well as outside according to uniform criteria

der Automobilindustrie allmählich Gestalt an. Konkret arbeitet Mercedes-Benz an dieser Strategie seit Mitte der neunziger Jahre.

Eine besondere Brisanz erfuhr das Thema der einheitlichen Gestaltung der Mercedes-Benz Markenplattformen jüngst durch veränderte gesetzliche Rahmenbedingungen im Bereich der Europäischen Union. Sie stellen das Verhältnis der Vertragshändler zu den Markenherstellern auf eine neue Basis, genauer: sie deregulieren es schrittweise. Mittelfristig können Vertragshändler und -werkstätten ihre Markenpartner und -angebote ganz nach eigenem Gutdünken wählen bzw. zusammenstellen.

Für das *Branding* ist diese Lockerung der gegenseitigen Bindung von Marke und Handel eine Herausforderung: Konsequente und durchgängige Markenkommunikation am *Point of Sale* ist in Zukunft nur gewährleistet, wenn der Automobilproduzent Plattformen für den Eigenvertrieb schaffen kann – und /oder über treue Händlernetze verfügt, die auch künftig bereit sind, mit dem Hersteller markenstrategisch an einem Strang zu ziehen. Infolgedessen plant Mercedes-Benz einerseits, in ausgewählten Märkten rund um den Globus den Fahrzeugvertrieb unter der Konzernregie von DaimlerChrysler auszubauen, andererseits unternimmt Mercedes-Benz große Anstrengungen, um die Vertragspartner in aller Welt bei der Gestaltung der Markenplattformen mit Rat und Tat fachmännisch zu unterstützen.

Ungeachtet aller modernen Markenstrategien und -aktivitäten ist das Prinzip der Funktionalität beim Bau von Autohäusern nach wie vor in Kraft. Strukturell prägend ist die Trias von Ausstellungsraum (Beratung/ Verkauf), Werkstatt (Service) und Teilelager (Logistik). Zum einen kommt es darauf an, diese Funktionsbereiche sinnvoll, effizient und kundenfreundlich zu verknüpfen, zum anderen ist stets eine Planfigur zu finden, die Spielräume lässt für Erweiterungen und eine Differenzierung der einzelnen Bereiche.

Diese fundamentale Planungslogik prägt alle Mercedes-Benz Autohäuser der jüngsten Generation. Im durchgängig angewandten Konzept des „Vertriebssterns" findet sie ihren räumlich-ökonomischen

and to characterise them with a brand identity on a worldwide scale. To be exact, Mercedes-Benz has been working on this strategy since the mid-nineties.

The subject of the uniform design of Mercedes-Benz brand platforms became particularly explosive recently due to legal guidelines that were changed in the area of the European Union. They place the relation between the appointed retailer and the brand manufacturer on a new footing. To be more precise, they deregulate it step by step. In the mid-term, appointed retailers and garages can select and put together their brand partners and offers at their own discretion.

This relaxation of mutual binding between the brand and trade is a challenge for *branding*: Consistent and constant brand communication at the *point of sale* is only guaranteed in the future if the automobile producer can create platforms for the sales of his own vehicles – and / or disposes over loyal dealer networks, who are also prepared to work with manufacturers in a market strategic way in the future. As a result of this Mercedes-Benz is planning, on the one hand, to extend vehicle sales under the concern directorship of DaimlerChrysler in selected markets around the globe; on the other hand, Mercedes-Benz is making a great effort to support sales partners all over the world in the design of brand platforms by offering them expert help and advice.

Despite all modern brand strategies and activities, the principle of functionality in the building of the car dealerships is still in force. Structurally characteristic is the triad of exhibition rooms (consultation/ sales), garage (service) and parts storeroom (logistics). On the one hand it is about linking these function areas sensibly, efficiently and in a customer-friendly way; on the other hand, a plan figure has to be constantly found to allow leeway for extensions and a differentiation of the single areas.

This fundamental planning logic has characterised all Mercedes-Benz car dealerships of recent generations. In the "sales star" – a concept that is consistently used – it is expressed in a spatial-economic way. The term marks every central area of the car dealership – the

Wo der Schreibtisch zur
Markenplattform wird:
Beratungszone im Autohaus

Where the desk becomes
a brand platform: consulting
zone in the showroom.

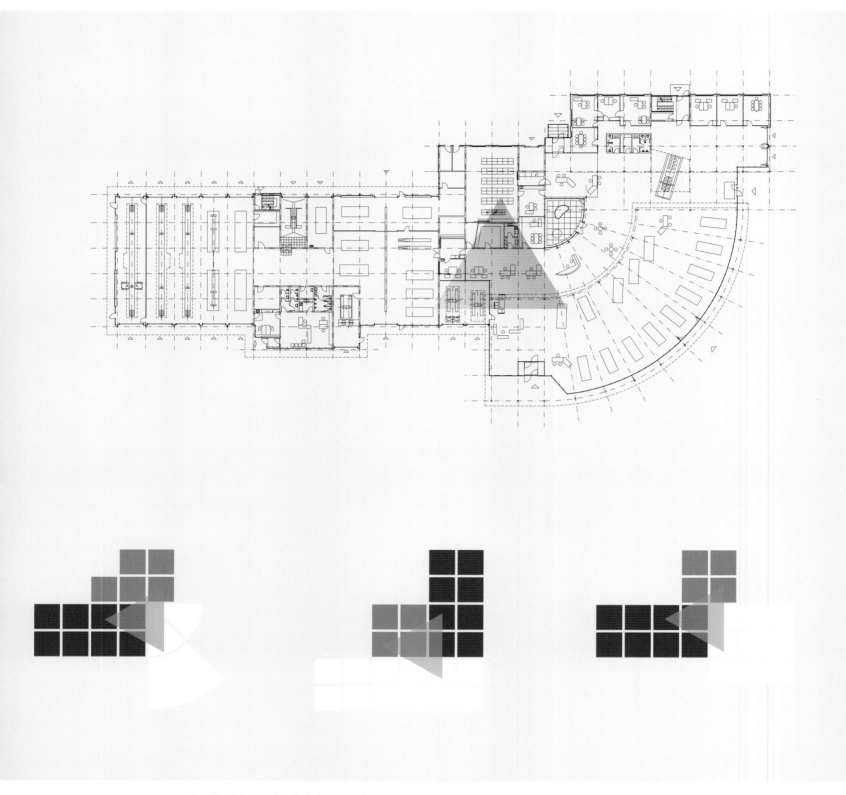

Der „Vertriebsstern" verknüpft
die Bereiche Ausstellung /
Beratung, Werkstatt / Kunden-
dienst und Lager / Ersatzteil-
verkauf in funktionaler Weise.

The "sales star" connects
the areas of exhibitions / consulting / garage / customer
service and storeroom /
replacement parts sales in
a functional way.

Ausdruck. Der Begriff kennzeichnet jenen zentralen Bereich des Autohauses, an dem die ersten substantiellen Kontakte mit dem Publikum stattfinden. Von hier aus erschließen sich den Kunden über kurze Wege alle relevanten Service-Bereiche: Ausstellung, Beratung, Verkauf und Finanzierung, Zubehör- und Ersatzteileverkauf, Kundendienstannahme, Fahrzeugauslieferung.

Die in der Figur des Vertriebssterns schon mitgedachte kreis- bzw. kugelsymmetrische Ordnung schafft Klarheit und Übersicht in jedem denkbaren architektonischen „Format". Darüber hinaus bürgt sie schon im Ansatz für die angestrebte strukturelle „Selbstähnlichkeit" der Mercedes-Benz Markenplattformen, ohne dabei eine (unerwünschte) Tendenz zur Uniformität zu erzeugen. In Kombination mit einem Regelwerk konstruktiver und (innen)architektonischer Detaillösungen entstand und entsteht nun schrittweise eine charakteristische Markenarchitektur, die weltweit

• allen Formaten des Mercedes-Benz Autohauses ein wiedererkennbares, einheitlich wirkendes Erscheinungsbild mit gleichwertigen Kommunikations- und Orientierungsmöglichkeiten verleiht,

• für die Anforderungen des Vertriebs und der Markenpräsentation jeweils triftige, und das heißt auch: ausgewogene Lösungen anbietet,

• den Qualitätsanspruch der Marke unabhängig vom Format in ästhetisch und funktional gleichwertiger, anspruchsvoller Weise in Architektur „übersetzt".

Die unterschiedlichen Autohaus-Kategorien im globalen Vertriebskonzept der Marke werden also unter dem Aspekt der Gestaltung weder privilegiert noch benachteiligt. Eine hierarchische Stufung der Typologie und der Raumprogramme ergibt sich allein auf der Basis unterschiedlicher jährlicher Absatzvolumina. Das kleinste Format ist das „Autohaus 500"; ihm folgen das „Autohaus 1000" und das „Autohaus 2000". Übertroffen werden diese Formate von den großen, metropolitanen „Mercedes-Benz Centern", in denen nicht nur die komplette Produktpalette von Mercedes-Benz Platz findet, sondern auch eine (in der Entwicklung befindliche) „Markengalerie". Unterschritten werden sie von so genannten

point at which the first substantial contact takes place with the public; from this point customers can reach all the relevant services areas in the shortest way: exhibition, consulting, sales and financing, accessories and spare parts, customer services application and vehicle delivery.

The circle or spherical-symmetrical order conceived in the figure of the sales star creates clarity and an overview in any thinkable architectonic "format". In addition to this, it guarantees from the start the desired structural "self-similarity" of the Mercedes-Benz brand platforms without creating an (unwelcome) tendency towards uniformity. In combination with the rules and regulations of constructive and (interior) architectural detail solutions, characteristic brand architecture developed and develops step by step, which on a worldwide scale

• lends all the types of Mercedes-Benz car dealership formats a recognisable, uniform appearance with the same opportunities of communication and orientation;

• offers convincing, and that also means balanced, solutions for sales requirements and presentation of the brand;

• "translates" the quality level of the brand independent of format in an equally aesthetic and functional way into the architecture at the highest standard.

So, viewed under this aspect of design the varying categories of car dealerships in the global sales concept of the brand are neither privileged nor disadvantaged. A hierarchy of typology and spatial programme only ensues on the basis of varying annual turnover. The smallest format is the car dealership "Car dealership 500"; this is followed by "Car dealership 1000" and the "Car dealership 2000". These formats are surpassed by the large metropolitan "Mercedes-Benz Centres", in which not only the complete spectrum of Mercedes-Benz products can be found but which also dispose over a Brand Gallery (still in the development stage). Falling short of these are the so-called "Mercedes-Benz spots", which as a rule are run as inner-city satellites of the Mercedes-Benz Centre.

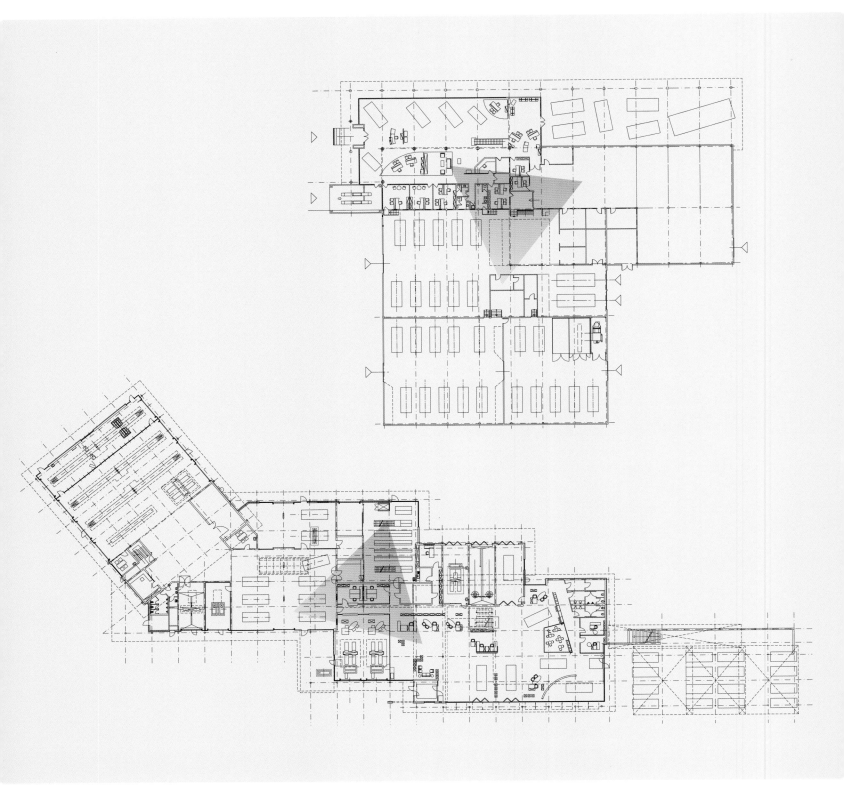

Mit dem „Vertriebsstern"
lassen sich zahlreiche
Varianten räumlicher Organisation konfigurieren.

Numerous variants of the
"sales star" can be configured
in the spatial organisation.

Die Funktionen des Mercedes-Benz Autohauses

„Mercedes-Benz Spots", die in der Regel als innerstädtische Satelliten der Mercedes-Benz Center betrieben werden.

Mit zunehmender Größe erfährt das Mercedes-Benz Autohaus eine funktionale Differenzierung vor allem im Ausstellungsbereich: Je mehr Platz hier zur Verfügung steht, desto mehr Möglichkeiten eröffnen sich für eine erlebnisorientierte Produkt- und Themendarstellung und für die Inszenierung der Marke selbst. Hier spielt auch das Merchandising von markenkompatiblen Accessoires eine wichtige Rolle, dem in allen Formaten eigene Flächen nach dem Shop-in-Shop-Prinzip gewidmet sind.

Die Präsentationsfläche im „Autohaus 500" bietet Raum für eine kleine Auswahl von Fahrzeugen und ein „Themenfeld"; im „Autohaus 1000" sind Flächen für einige Themenfelder vorhanden; im „Autohaus 2000" ist die Zahl der Themenfelder deutlich erhöht, außerdem lässt sich hier unter bestimmten Voraussetzungen auch das Volumen einer architektonisch hervorgehobenen „Markengalerie" in den Bau integrieren.

Das Sonderformat der Mercedes-Benz Center bietet, wie angedeutet, Raum für die gesamte Produktpalette der Marke und darüber hinaus für größere Veranstaltungen („Events"). Die Markengalerie ist integraler Bestandteil dieses Großformats, das im Übrigen auch besondere Anforderungen an seine architektonische Differenzierung und städtebauliche Ausprägung im urbanen Umfeld stellt.

With increasing size the Mercedes-Benz car dealership experiences a functional differentiation, above all in the exhibition area: The more space is available, the more opportunities arise for experience-orientated product and theme presentations as well as for the stage-management of the brand itself. The merchandising of brand-compatible accessories also plays an important role here, as an area is dedicated to this according to the "shop-in-shop principle".

The presentation area in "Car dealership 500" offers space for a small selection of vehicles and a theme area; in the "Car dealership 1000" there are surfaces available for several theme areas; in "Car dealership 2000" the amount of theme areas is significantly higher, and apart from that under certain conditions it is possible to integrate the space of an architectonically underlined Brand Gallery into the building.

The special format of the Mercedes-Benz Centre offers, as indicated, space for the brand's complete spectrum of products and, in addition to this, space for larger events. The Brand Gallery is an integral part of this large format, which by the way also makes particular demands on its architectural differentiation and urban character in urban surroundings.

Autohaus-Design als Element
der Markenstrategie
Car dealership design as an element
of the brand strategy

Charakteristische Regeldetails sorgen weltweit für ein einheitliches Erscheinungsbild der Mercedes-Benz Architektur: Autohaus in Schwäbisch Hall

Characteristic stipulation details ensure a consistent appearance of Mercedes-Benz architecture on a worldwide scale: showroom in Schwäbisch Hall.

Autohaus-Design als Element der Markenstrategie

Autohaus-Design als Element der Markenstrategie

Die Eindrücke, die Gefühle und das Begehren, die das Markenprodukt Automobil und insbesondere natürlich die Fahrzeuge der Premium-Klasse Mercedes-Benz auf der Straße und in Bewegung leicht selbst mobilisieren können, müssen in der Sphäre des Autohauses in anderer Weise und mit gänzlich anderen Mitteln erzeugt, zumindest thematisiert werden.

Im Autohaus werden Fahrzeuge zu Skulpturen, wird die Welt zur Galerie. Parkett ersetzt das Band der Straße. Horizont und Himmel verwandeln sich in Mauern, Decken und *Curtain Walls*. Und statt jenes raumgreifenden *Road Movies*, in das sich der Besucher vielleicht gerne hineinträumen würde, ist auf einer ziemlich überschaubaren Bühne eine Szene zu gestalten, in der eher stille Helden ihren Auftritt haben: Autos in selbstvergessener Ruhe, technische Daten aus dem Innenleben der Maschinen, Ausstattungsdetails und Materialmuster. Und natürlich, allgegenwärtig, die Marke.

Nach Gablers Wirtschaftslexikon ist eine Marke zunächst nicht mehr als ein „Name, Zeichen, Design, Symbol oder eine Kombination dieser Elemente": ein Abstraktum also, das anschaulich, konkret und „sprechend" nur werden kann im Dialog mit jenen Dingen, auf die es verweist und die im Gegenzug der Marke sinnfällig Ausdruck und Inhalt verleihen.

Macht man sich diese Perspektive zu Eigen, stellt das dreidimensionale Erscheinungsbild des *Point of Sale* – mithin das architektonische Design des Autohauses – eine erste, wichtige Benutzeroberfläche der Marke dar. Sie akzentuiert die „Haltung" der Marke und wird somit unmittelbar Bestandteil sowohl der Marken- wie auch der dahinter stehenden Unternehmenskultur. Natürlich übertrifft die Mercedes-Benz Markenwelt mit all ihren subtilen Konnotationen und Gefühlsdimensionen die kommerziell geprägte Welt des Autohauses an Komplexität. Aber das Mercedes-Benz Autohaus ist doch immer auch repräsentatives Modell dieser Markenwelt: nämlich die notwendigerweise vereinfachte und bis zu einem gewissen Grad auch standardisierte Metaphrase aller Markenwerte und -versprechen.

Car dealership design as an element of the brand strategy

The impressions, feelings, and desires which are all easily aroused by the brand product automobile and in particular, of course, by the vehicles of the premium class Mercedes-Benz, on the road and in motion, have to be created in another way using completely different means in the sphere of the car dealership. Or at least they have to be made into a theme.

In the car dealership vehicles become sculptures; the world becomes a gallery. Parquet replaces the strip of road. The horizon and sky are transformed into walls, ceilings and *curtain walls*. And instead of each space-occupying *road movie*, which visitors would perhaps like to dream along to, a scene is to be set on a relatively moderate stage. A scene in which rather calm heroes take the stage: cars in self-denying quiet, technical data from the interior life of a machine, furnishing details and material samples. And, of course, the brand omnipresent, as always.

According to Gabler's economic dictionary, the brand is, at first, no more than a "name, sign, design, symbol or a combination of these elements": thus an abstract, which can only be vivid, definite and "speaking" in dialogue with all the things that refer to it and which in a countermove lends the brand obvious expression and content.

If this perspective is made too peculiar, the three-dimensional appearance of the *point of sale* – consequently the architectonic design of the car dealership – represents a significant initial user interface of the brand. It accentuates the "attitude" of the brand and therefore becomes an integral part of the brand as well as the company culture behind this. With all its subtle connotations and dimensions of feeling, the Mercedes-Benz obviously surpasses the commercially characterised world of car dealerships as far as complexity is concerned. But the Mercedes-Benz car dealership is however also a representative model of this brand world: namely, as the necessitated simplified, and to a certain degree, standardised meta-phrase of all brand values and promises.

Es ist nicht möglich, den kompliziert aufgebauten Katalog der Markenwerte von Mercedes-Benz hier erschöpfend zu behandeln. Einige Schlüsselbegriffe mögen deshalb genügen, um die Ableitung der architektonischen und stilistischen Leitbilder und ihre Umsetzung in Regeldetails für die verschiedenen Formate der Mercedes-Benz Autohäuser aus diesem Wertekatalog zu skizzieren.

Die Markenidentität von Mercedes-Benz basiert auf einem mehrdimensionalen Wertesystem, dessen Grundgefüge festgelegt ist, das aber doch inhaltlich ständig dynamisch weiterentwickelt werden muss. Nur so lässt sich der anspruchsvolle Marken-Claim „Mercedes-Benz. Die Zukunft des Automobils" einlösen.

In diesem Wertgefüge dominieren die „Grundwerte" der Marke – etwa Qualität, Zuverlässigkeit, Sicherheit, Komfort. Ergänzt werden sie durch „Trendwerte", die das Potential der Marke in Sachen Stil, Design und Fahrvergnügen markieren; ferner durch „Orientierungswerte" – sie reflektieren den Bezug der Marke zum Prinzip Verantwortung und zum Wertekanon der sie tragenden Gesellschaft(en).

Es versteht sich, dass dieses Wertesystem in erster Linie auf die Produkte der Marke, nämlich auf Automobile, das mobilitätsbezogene Dienstleistungsportfolio und damit auch auf die Realitäten dieses Marktsegments gemünzt ist. Für die markenkonforme Planung und Gestaltung einer neuen Generation von Autohaus-Formaten musste der Wertekatalog von Mercedes-Benz also „übersetzt", d.h. der Prozess- und Funktionslogik sowohl des Bauens, des Fahrzeugvertriebs wie eben auch der Marken- und Kundenkommunikation angepasst werden.

Bei dieser „Übersetzung" des Markenprofils in die Sprache der Architektur spielte der Katalog der Grund- und Orientierungswerte von Mercedes-Benz eine gewichtigere Rolle als die Trendwerte. Dafür gibt es simple Gründe: Zum einen sind Lebensdauer und Investitionsvolumen bei Bauwerken deutlich länger bzw. größer als bei Kraftfahrzeugen. Zum anderen wird es Jahre dauern, bis im weltweit verzweigten Mercedes-Benz Vertrieb mit seinen 6.000 Autohäusern eine neue Generation von Bauten tatsächlich

It is not possible to exhaustively deal with the complicatedly established catalogue of Mercedes-Benz brand values here. A few key terms may therefore be sufficient to illustrate the different formats of Mercedes-Benz car dealership buildings based on this value system and realised according to architectonic and stylistic guidelines as well as their specific realisation in keeping with detailed regulations.

The Mercedes-Benz brand identity is based on a variously facetted system of values, the basis of which has been stipulated but the contents of which still have to be dynamically developed further on a continual basis. It is thus for this reason alone that the high-quality brand slogan "Mercedes-Benz. The future of automobiles" can be upheld.

In the framework of these values the "basic values" of the brand dominate – such as quality, reliability, safety and comfort. These are complemented via the "trend values" which mark the potential of the brand in aspects such as style, design and driving pleasure; and furthermore by "orientation values" – these reflect the relation of the brand to the principle of responsibility and to the values of the societies they are based on.

It goes without saying that this value system is primarily aimed at the products of the brand, namely the automobile, the mobility-related service portfolio and along with this at the realities of the market segment. So, for the brand conformed planning and design of the new generation of car dealership formats, the Mercedes-Benz value catalogue has to be "translated", this means the process- and function-logistics as well as building, car sales and the brand- customer-communication all have to be adapted.

The catalogue of Mercedes-Benz basic and orientation values play a more important role than the trend value in this "translation" of the brand profile into the language of architecture. There are simple reasons for this: Firstly, the life span and volume of investment in construction work is considerably longer and larger than in motor vehicles. Secondly, it will take years until a new generation of buildings has actually become the visual characteristic in the worldwide

Transparenz ist ein dominantes
Gestaltungsprinzip über alle
Retail-Formate hinweg: Beispiel
San Salvador

Transparency is a dominant
design principle in all the retail
formats: example San Salvador.

bildprägend geworden ist. Die Entscheidung für ein flexibles, hochwertiges aber nicht extravagantes, tendenziell zeitlos und sachlich wirkendes Architekturkonzept erscheint deshalb geradezu zwingend.

Das architektonische Regelwerk für die Autohausformate von Mercedes-Benz lässt Spielraum für viele individuelle Lösungen, auch im Kontext von Umbauten oder der Erweiterung von Bestandsbauten. Unter diesem Aspekt folgt es übrigens den Trendwerten der Marke. Im Farbkonzept für die Innenraumgestaltung und in der Entscheidung, der neuen Generation der Mercedes-Benz Autohäuser im Kunden- und Ausstellungsbereich durch verglaste Fassaden Transparenz und Großzügigkeit zu verleihen, werden als räumliche Metaphern die Trendwerte sinnfällig.

Im Ganzen hingegen ist das Erscheinungsbild, welches die architektonischen Regeldetails erzeugen, an der Skala der Grundwerte orientiert: Die neuen Autohäuser von Mercedes-Benz wirken innen und außen durch die Betonung konstruktiver Elemente gleichermaßen solide wie „technisch". Dabei sorgt das dem Konzept unterlegte Entwurfssystem für elegante Konturen, filigrane Lineamente und eine bisweilen „klassische" Rhythmisierung der Baukörper.

Der disziplinierte Einsatz von Baustoffen und sonstigen Materialien sowie die Infrastruktur für das technische und energetische Gebäudemanagement spiegeln wiederum – wenngleich für Architektur-Laien naturgemäß schwer erkennbar – die Orientierungswerte der Marke wider. Einen hohen Stellenwert genießen unter diesem Aspekt auch die städtebaulich sensible Dimensionierung und Positionierung der Baukörper sowie die Gestaltung der Freiflächen: eine besondere Qualität vor allem im Kontext der weltweit verbreiteten Praxis, Industriebauten im Weichbild der Städte ohne Rücksicht auf das jeweilige Umfeld aus dem Boden zu stampfen.

Der Katalog der explizit architektonischen Regeldetails für die neue Generation der Mercedes-Benz Autohäuser konzentriert sich auf Elemente, welche die Wiedererkennbarkeit der Bauten weltweit und formatübergreifend sicherstellen. Lässt man das strukturelle Konzept des „Vertriebssterns" und das

branches of Mercedes-Benz sales with its 6,000 car dealerships. The decision to create a flexible, valuable but not extravagant practical looking architectural concept, which also tends to be timeless, therefore seems to be urgent.

The book of architectural regulations on the Mercedes-Benz car dealership formats allows leeway for individual solutions even in the context of conversions or in extensions of component buildings. By the way, this aspect follows the trend values of the brand. In the customer and exhibition area, the choice of colour concept, the interior design and the decision to lend the new generation of Mercedes-Benz car dealerships transparency and spaciousness using glassed façades are obvious as spatial metaphors of the trend values.

However, as a whole the appearance created by the architectonic specification details, is oriented towards the scale of basic values: On the outside and on the inside the new Mercedes-Benz car dealerships appear equally solid and "technical" due to the emphasis on constructive elements. In this the design system, which underlies the concept, ensures elegant contours, filigree lineaments and, now and then, a "classical" rhythmically-made structure.

The disciplined use of building materials and other materials, as well as the infrastructure of the technical and energetic building management, in turn mirrors the orientation values of the brand – although this is naturally difficult to recognise for architectural laypeople. Under this aspect, high value is placed on the urban dimensioning being sensitively realised as well as the positioning of the building bodies and the design of the free spaces. This is a special quality, above all, in the context of the worldwide practice of building industrial buildings overnight and placing them into the soft scenery of towns whilst completely ignoring their surroundings.

The catalogue of explicit architectonic specification details for a new generation of Mercedes-Benz car dealerships concentrates on elements which guarantee the recognition value and general format of buildings worldwide. If we leave aside for a moment the structural concept of the "sales star" and the design system,

Betont konstruktiv, aber zurückhaltend: Das System-Design der Stützen und Träger gibt der Architektur eine technoide Note.

Purposely constructive but reserved: The system design of the beams and supports lends the architecture a technoid note.

Nicht nur die blauen Stahl-
stützen vor den gläsernen
Curtain Walls, sondern auch
eingefärbte Betonwände
modulieren das Erscheinungsbild der Autohausfassaden.

It is not only the blue steel
supports in front of the glass
curtain walls but also the
coloured cement walls that
modulate the appearance
of the showroom façades.

Autohaus-Design als Element der Markenstrategie

Entwurfssystem, welches die Anwendung und den Einsatz der Elemente determiniert, einmal beiseite, so handelt es sich um folgende Themen: Farbe und Form der Außenstützen an den Hauptfassaden, das Design der Dachüberstände, -kanten und -träger, das System der wandhohen Stahl-/Glasfassaden mit den optional eingestellten Wandscheiben, das Thema „Portal", die Gestaltung der Werkstattfassaden und architektonische Lösungen für die „Markengalerien" der großen Autohausformate.

Die architektonische Hülle der Mercedes-Benz Autohäuser wirkt in ihrer Betonung des Konstruktiven technoid, wenn sie auch bewusst vermeidet, die derzeit modischen Stilmerkmale von „High Tech" explizit zum Thema zu machen: Die Bauten wollen schließlich nicht von Zeitgeistarchitektur erzählen, sondern von der Marke Mercedes-Benz. Erzeugt wird dennoch eine „coole" Grundstimmung, die der Besucher zunächst in das Gebäude mitnimmt. Dort allerdings wird die Atmosphäre durch Innenarchitektur, Mobiliar, Farb- und Lichtdesign sowie Medien so variantenreich „moduliert", dass die Markenplattform „Autohaus" sich dem interessierten Kunden schließlich als ein Ganzes darbietet. Auch für diese auf den Innenraum bezogenen Gestaltungsaufgaben existieren Konzepte, Vorgaben und Standards, auf die in weiteren Abschnitten des Buchs eingegangen wird.

Wie tief das Publikum jeweils in die Mercedes-Welt eintauchen kann, hängt von den örtlichen Ausstellungs- und Präsentationsmöglichkeiten ab. Je kleiner die Formate der Autohäuser sind, desto stärker müssen sie auf die Anliegen des Vertriebs ausgerichtet sein; mit zunehmender Größe gewinnt der Aspekt der Themendarstellung und der Markenpräsentation an Gewicht und Bedeutung.

Primäres Ziel ist allerdings, die Markenwelt von Mercedes-Benz in jedem Autohaus-Format als Integral zu kommunizieren – als Einheit von Produkten, Service und Kommunikation. Die Architektur übernimmt dabei die entscheidende, nämlich die intermediäre Funktion.

which determines the application and use of elements, we are dealing with the following themes. They concern the colour and shape of the outer pillars of the main façades, the design of the roof projections, edges and supports, the system of steel/glass façades at wall height with the optionally set glass walls, the theme of the "portal", the design of garage façades and architectonic solutions for the Brand Gallery in the large car dealership formats.

The architectonic shell of Mercedes-Benz car dealerships seems technoid as they underline the constructive, even if they consciously avoid turning the current fashionable trend of "high tech" explicitly into a theme: In the end, the buildings do not want to express zeitgeist architecture, they want to express the Mercedes-Benz brand. Nevertheless a "cool" basic atmosphere is created, which initially attracts visitors into the building. However, here the atmosphere is so "modulated" in many variations by the interior architecture, furnishing, colour and light design as well as media that the brand platform of a car dealership is finally presented to interested customers as a whole. Even for the design tasks related to the inner rooms, there are concepts, stipulations and standards, which will be outlined more fully in further sections of the book.

Exactly how deep the public can dive into each Mercedes world directly depends on the exhibition and presentation possibilities on site. The smaller the format of the car dealership, the more it has to be aligned to sales demands: The aspect of theme and brand presentation gain weight and significance with increasing size.

However, the primary goal is to communicate the Mercedes-Benz brand world as integral in every car dealership – as a unity of products, services and communication. The architecture takes over the decisive, that is, intermediary function in this.

mit dem ein

Der erste Mercedes, für viele Experten
Automobil, legte im März 1901 auf den
großartige Premiere hin. Wilhelm Maybe
konstruiert. Leider existiert heute kein E
35 PS Fahrzeug, wohl aber vom direkten N
Mercedes-Simplex des Jahres 1902, d

Markenprägung und Markenerlebnis:
Die „Brand Gallery"
Brand characterisation and brand experience:
the "Brand Gallery"

Rund ist der Markenkern:
die „Brand Gallery" in CAD-
Darstellung

The brand nucleus is round:
the "Brand Gallery" as a
CAD depiction.

Markenprägung und Markenerlebnis:
Die „Brand Gallery"

Im letzten Jahrzehnt wurde den Marken eine gesteigerte Aufmerksamkeit zuteil. Vor allem die Finanzwelt und speziell die Investmentbanken interessierten sich für ihr Wertschöpfungspotential und entwickelten allerlei Methoden, jenes exakt zu berechnen.

Im gleichen Zeitraum allerdings änderten sich auch einige Parameter der Markenökonomie: Die Marktforschung registrierte auf der Kundenseite eine generelle Abnahme der Markenloyalität und ein verändertes Konsumverhalten – die Käufer entscheiden sich zunehmend spontaner und zeigen sich erlebnishungriger. Speziell die Automobilwirtschaft musste zur Kenntnis nehmen, dass Markenstrategien, die sich allein auf Produkte und eine produktorientierte Markenprofilierung stützten, nicht mehr zufriedenstellend funktionierten.

In der Folge entwickelte die Automobilwirtschaft rund um ihre *Product Brands* einen Kranz von Aktivitäten, die den Kunden neue Markenerlebnisse vermittelten. Dazu gehören etwa innovative Dienstleistungsangebote – *Service Brands* – und der Aufbau von Markenzentren, die den Zielgruppen individuelle Erfahrungen und „Begegnungen" mit der Marke bieten sollen. Das konzeptionelle Handwerkszeug zur Neugestaltung solcher Markenerlebnisse war den Unternehmen zur Hand: Sie stützten und stützen sich auf praktische Erfahrungen aus dem Bereich der Messekommunikation. Messeplaner, Ausstellungsarchitekten und Event-Spezialisten wissen genau, wie man Produkte in Szene setzt, technische Innovationen in Themenausstellungen an Laien vermittelt und faszinierende Markenwelten synästhetisch und multimedial auf engstem Raum unterbringt.

Mercedes-Benz blieb von diesen Trends nicht unberührt. Beflügelt von spektakulären Erfolgen mit temporären Markenplattformen auf den internationalen Automessen, trat man entschlossen in den anhebenden Wettbewerb um erlebnisorientierte Markenkommunikation im regulären Vertriebssystem ein. Im Gleichtakt mit der Formulierung eines durchgängigen Architekturkonzepts für die Autohausformate entwickelten die

Brand characterisation and brand experience:
The "Brand Gallery"

In the last decade attention has increasingly turned towards brands. The finance sector and investment banks in particular have taken an interest in the value-adding potential of branding and have developed various quantifying methods to measure this accurately.

However, at the same time, some parameters of the brand economy have changed: Market research has registered a general decline in customer brand loyalty and a change in consumer behaviour – for example, consumers now make increasingly spontaneous choices and show a greater willingness to experience new things. The car industry in particular has come to realise that brand strategies concentrating solely on products and product-orientated brand profiling are no longer sufficient.

As a result, the car industry has developed a whole circle of activities around their *product brands*, which have been able to deliver new brand experiences to their customers. These include, for example, innovative service offers – *service brands* – and the development of brand centres, which are designed to offer the target groups individual experiences and "encounters" with the brand. The conceptual tools for the redesign of such brand experiences were already made available to the companies: They base and based them on practical experiences from the trade fair communications sector. Trade fair planners, exhibition architects and event specialists know exactly how to orchestrate the presentation of a product, how to educate laypeople about technical innovations through themed exhibitions, and how to present fascinating brand universes through syneasthetical experiences and multimedia in confined spaces.

Mercedes-Benz has not been left untouched by these trends. Encouraged by spectacular successes with temporary brand platforms at international car fairs, they decisively joined an increasingly fierce competition, which integrates experience-orientated brand communication into their regular sales strategy. Parallel to the development of consistent architectural concepts for car showrooms, brand strategists

Markenstrategen Ideen zur erlebnis- und themenorientierten Produktpräsentation in den größeren Häusern.

Spektakulärstes Produkt dieser Entwicklungsarbeit ist die Markengalerie (*Brand Gallery*). Sie wird architektonisch und funktional zentraler Bestandteil der in Planung befindlichen Mercedes-Benz Center in den europäischen Metropolen werden. Konzipiert als wuchtiger Kegelstumpf, der vom Mercedesstern bekrönt ist, setzt dieser Baukörper jeweils einen markanten städtebaulichen Akzent im Komplex der Center, da diese prinzipiell aus einzelnen (und niedrigeren) Gebäuden zusammengefügt sind.

Der Markengalerie fällt nicht nur die Rolle eines Ausstellungsgebäudes zu, in dem markenrelevante Schwerpunktthemen inszeniert werden. Sie verbindet und erschließt auch die um sie herum gruppierten Gebäudekomplexe und Funktionsbereiche. Ihre Architektur erhält dadurch eine metaphorische Qualität: Die Markengalerie wird buchstäblich zum „Markenkern".

Mit der Markengalerie wird ein Dilemma aus der Welt der großen Mercedes-Benz Autohäuser geschafft, das in den kleineren Formaten wohl noch längere Zeit virulent bleiben wird. Gemeint sind die konkurrierenden Raumansprüche einerseits der „traditionellen" produkt- und informationsorientierten Präsentationspraxis, andererseits die der strategisch motivierten Inszenierung von markenbezogenen Erlebnis- und Kommunikationsräumen.

Die Markengalerie ist der Ort, an dem Geschichten erzählt werden. Hier geht es um Kommunikation auf der Ebene der Gefühle – und um eine emotional geprägte Ausformulierung des Markenbilds. In der Markengalerie treten die Interessen des Vertriebs in den Hintergrund. Das Publikum ist nicht hier, um Informationen für eine Kaufentscheidung zu sammeln – es soll ganz zwanglos in die Marke „eintauchen" und dabei Spaß haben: Mercedes-Benz Kunden, Fremdkunden, Sympathisanten der Marke, Neugierige, Technikfreaks, Kinder und Jugendliche.

Kommuniziert werden in der Markengalerie Botschaften mit Faszinationspotential. Transportiert werden sie in Wanderausstellungen, die turnusmäßig wechseln

developed ideas for experience or theme-orientated product presentations in the bigger car dealerships.

The most spectacular result of this development work is the *Brand Gallery*. Architecturally and functionally it will become the central part of the Mercedes-Benz Centres currently planned in European metropolitan cities. In the shape of a massive cone stump, crowned by the Mercedes star, the building creates a strong urban profile within the centre, which consists mainly of separate low-rise buildings.

The Brand Gallery will not only play the role of an exhibition hall, where themes relevant to the brand will be staged. It is also to link and access the building complexes and functional areas grouped around it. Its architecture thus attains a metaphorical quality: The Brand Gallery literally becomes the "brand core".

The Brand Gallery will eliminate the dilemma of the big Mercedes-Benz car dealerships, something which will probably persist in smaller car dealerships for a considerable amount of time. Principally this refers, on the one hand, to the competing demands for space by the "traditional" product and information-orientated presentation techniques, and, on the other hand, to those of a strategically motivated staging of brand-related experience and communication spaces.

The Brand Gallery is a place where stories are told. The communication works on an emotional level, and the emotional characterisation of the brand image is of utmost importance. Interests relating to sales objectives are not the focus of the Brand Gallery. The audience is not here to gather information needed prior to a purchase decision, but should "immerse" itself freely in the brand – and have fun: Mercedes-Benz clients, other clients, brand sympathisers, curious technical wizards, children and young people.

The Brand Gallery communicates messages with a potential for fascination. They are carried through in regularly changing moving exhibitions and circulate in the network of brand platforms. Some of these exhibitions will be produced for car fairs, which have been adapted to the Brand Galleries. As their spaces are standardised, their networked brand

Die Standardisierung der Markengalerien in den Mercedes-Benz Centern ermöglicht es, Ausstellungen weltweit in bester Qualität und dennoch ökonomisch zu organisieren.

The standardisation of the Brand Galleries in the Mercedes-Benz Centres enables exhibitions to be organised on a worldwide scale to the highest standard but also economically.

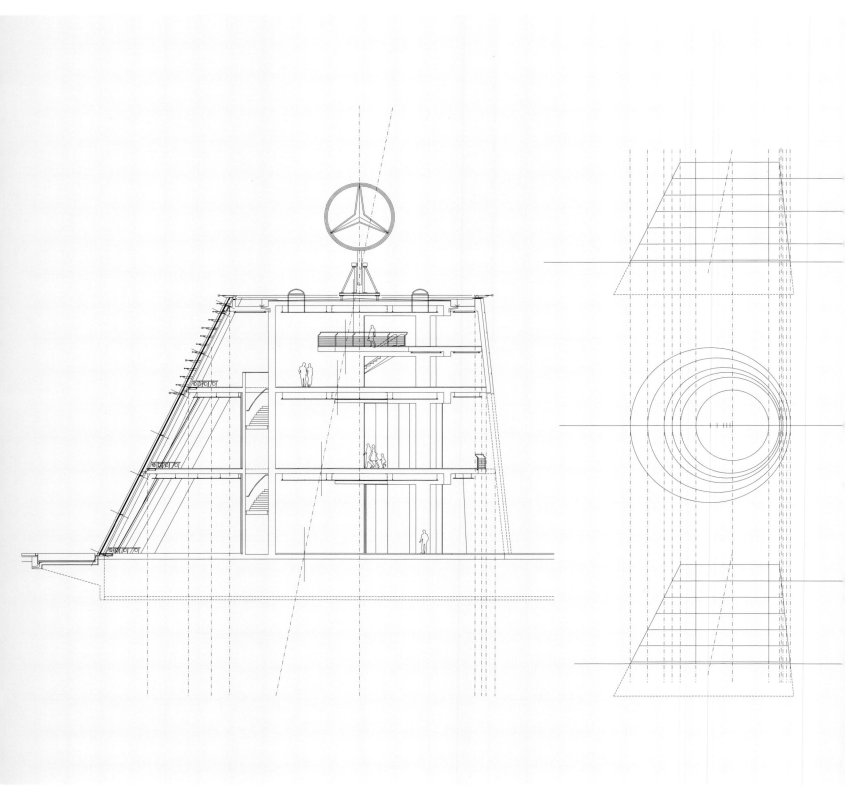

**Die räumliche Struktur
im Querschnitt**

Cross-section of the spatial
structure

Markenprägung und Markenerlebnis: Die „Brand Gallery"

und im Netz der Markenplattformen zirkulieren. Bei manchen dieser Ausstellungen wird es sich um Produktionen für Automobilmessen handeln, die den Gegebenheiten der Markengalerien angepasst wurden. Da deren Räumlichkeiten standardisiert sind, lässt sich die weltweit vernetzte Markenkommunikation bei höchstem Qualitätsstandard der Ausstellungen dennoch effizient und ökonomisch gestalten.

Das Spektrum an Themen, die geeignet sind, in der Markengalerie publikumswirksam inszeniert zu werden, ist breit. „Dauerbrenner" sind etwa die Markengeschichte, Forschungs- und Entwicklungsthemen und der Motorsport. Für den Wechselausstellungsbetrieb eignen sich Themen wie z.B. Mercedes-Benz Design, Sicherheit oder spezielle Fahrzeuglegenden. Mit der Vorstellung von Produktneuheiten und mit markenkompatiblen Fremdausstellungen (z.B. Kunst, Mode, Wissenschaftsthemen) lassen sich gesellschaftliche Ereignisse inszenieren, die neue Besuchergruppen anziehen.

Mittel- und langfristig wird sich erweisen, ob ein Erlebnisraum wie die Markengalerie mit Hilfe neuer Medien und Darstellungstechniken virtualisiert, damit verkleinert und so etwa tauglich für kleinere Autohausformate gemacht werden kann. Entscheidende Kriterien sind der Erhalt bzw. der Verlust des „authentischen" Markenerlebnisses im Mediengebrauch – und eben die Frage, welche Entwicklungen der Wandel der Medienkultur zeitigen wird.

Auch die Mercedes-Benz Markengalerien sind Medienräume, deren Ausstattung mit der Technik jeweils Schritt halten wird. Im Übrigen sind die Markengalerien nicht am Reißbrett entworfen worden, sondern unter anderem im „Mercedes-Benz Markenstudio", das über ein Virtual-Reality-Labor verfügt. Das Konzept wurde unter Einsatz digitaler Modelle Schritt für Schritt optimiert – ganz im Sinne der authentischen Markenkommunikation.

communications can be implemented efficiently and economically worldwide with the highest exhibition quality standards.

There is a wide range of themes, which can be orchestrated effectively to the public in the Brand Gallery. "All time favourites" are brand history, research and development themes and motor sports. Themes such as Mercedes-Benz design, safety or special legendary models are best suited to the changing exhibitions. Via the presentation of product innovations and external exhibitions (i.e. art, fashion, science) society events can be staged, which attract new visitor groups.

In the mid- and long-term it will become clear whether an experimental space like the Brand Gallery will be virtualised through media and art forms, or miniaturised and therefore become adaptable for smaller car dealerships. The decisive factors will be the preservation or loss of the "authentic" brand experience in the use of media and questions such as the kind of developments the changing media culture will undergo.

The Mercedes-Benz Brand Galleries are also media spaces, whose equipment has to be kept in sync with the latest technology. Besides, the Brand Galleries have not been designed at the drawing table but, amongst other places, in the "Mercedes-Benz brand studio", which has a virtual reality lab. The concept was optimised step by step using digital models – completely in line with authentic brand communication techniques.

Licht- und Farbdesign
Light and colour design

Wo Tages- und Kunstlicht sich vermischen, wird Licht- und Farbdesign zur Herausforderung.

Lighting and colour design become a challenge where daylight and artificial light merge.

Licht- und Farbdesign

Zum Ruhm des Architekten Le Corbusier hat nicht zuletzt eine griffige Definition von Architektur beigetragen, die wegen ihrer genialen Verkürzung auch heute noch gerne verwendet wird. Architektur, so stellte der Altmeister der Klassischen Moderne fest, sei „das Spiel der Formen im Licht".

Natürlich wusste auch Le Corbusier, dass Architektur weit mehr ist als das Arrangement von Baukörpern unter der Sonne. Aber das populär gewordene Zitat weist immerhin zutreffend auf die große Bedeutung der Lichtregie in der Baukunst hin.

Die von natürlicher und künstlicher Beleuchtung erzeugte Anmutung von Materialien und vor allem auch die auftretenden Farbreflexe beeinflussen ganz wesentlich die emotionale Wirkung von Baukörpern, Innenräumen und den sich darin befindenden Gegenständen. Mit anderen Worten – aus Licht und der Farbe von Oberflächen entsteht „Atmosphäre".

In einem Gebäude, das der Ausstellung und dem Verkauf von Automobilen dient, spielt Atmosphäre eine ganz besonders wichtige Rolle, und damit auch das Licht und die Farben im Kunden- und Ausstellungsbereich. Wenn schon das Spiel der Formen im Licht die Baukunst ausmachen soll, so trifft diese Definition fast noch mehr dort zu, wo es um Produktgestaltung geht, das bedeutet in diesem Fall: um die Wirkung des Designs von Fahrzeugen. Am Point of Sale ist Design definierbar als das Spiel der Karosserieformen unter natürlichem und künstlichem Licht.

Bei der Planung und Realisierung der kleinen und großen Autohäuser von Mercedes-Benz haben Lichtregie und Farbdesign deshalb einen außerordentlich hohen Stellenwert. Es gilt, einerseits die ausgestellten Fahrzeuge durch optimale Ausleuchtung wirksam und augenfällig zu inszenieren, andererseits soll sich das Autohaus insgesamt dem Kunden als „Wohlfühlraum" präsentieren, als Ambiente, das zu jeder Tages- und Nachtzeit und innen wie außen gleichermaßen Vertrauen und Neugier wecken kann.

Light and colour design

The fame of the architect Le Corbusier was partially due to his compact definition of architecture, which is still very much in use today. According to this master of classic modernism, architecture is "the learned game of forms assembled in the light".

Of course, Le Corbusier knew all too well that architecture was much more than simply forms assembled under the sun. However, this popular quotation correctly highlights the huge importance of good lighting in the art of architecture.

The effect that natural and artificial light, and especially colour reflections, have on materials significantly influences the emotional impact of buildings, interior spaces and the objects inside them. In other words – the light and colour of surfaces create an "atmosphere".

In a building used to exhibit and sell cars, atmosphere plays a particularly important role, therefore the choice of light and colours in the customer and exhibition areas is crucial. If the game of forms assembled in the light defines architecture, this definition is even more pertinent to product design, or car design in this case. At the point of sale, design can be defined as the game of bodywork forms in natural and artificial light.

Lighting and colour design are given an extraordinarily high status when planning and creating small and large Mercedes-Benz car showrooms. On the one hand, through the use of optimal lighting the exhibited vehicles should be staged effectively and their impact should be immediate; on the other hand, the showroom should be perceived by clients as a "feel-good area", an ambient space, which establishes trust and raises curiosity by night and day, inside and outside.

At first, the constraints of a building such as a car showroom do not encourage an expressive and atmospheric use of lighting. The explicitly transparent architecture of car showrooms and their

Dabei kommen die Eigentümlichkeiten des Bautyps Autohaus den Erfordernissen einer stimmungsvollen, ausdrucksstarken Aus- und Beleuchtung zunächst einmal keineswegs entgegen. Die betont transparente Architektur von Autohäusern und deren typischerweise große Glasfronten schaffen alles andere als „kontrollierte" Lichtverhältnisse: Je nach Wetter und Sonneneinstrahlung spiegeln die Fensterflächen – von außen betrachtet – eher die Umgebung der Bauten, als dass sie wirkungsvolle Einblicke in die innenräumlichen Ausstellungszonen gestatteten. Im Innern schließlich entsteht an den Fensterfronten – also im bevorzugten Exponatbereich – durch die von Minute zu Minute wechselnde Mischung aus gerichtetem Tageslicht und diffusem Kunstlicht eine nicht leicht zu beherrschende Situation, die oft eher den Anforderungen einer atmosphärischen Raumbeleuchtung gerecht wird als denen einer optimierten Fahrzeugbeleuchtung.

Immerhin sind Automobile die „Hauptdarsteller" im Autohaus, ihre Inszenierung hat Priorität. Fahrzeugkonturen müssen in ihren Schwüngen elegant und wirkungsvoll zur Geltung gebracht werden, Lackflächen sollen anmutig schimmern und dabei möglichst wenig Lichtreflexe spiegeln. Das Umfeld der Fahrzeuge soll möglichst blendfrei sein, wobei das „atmosphärische" Licht der Kundenzone wiederum nicht die Effekte der Fahrzeugbeleuchtung in ihrer Wirkung mindern darf.

Im Gegensatz zur „Black-Box-Situation", wie sie etwa auf Messen und Ausstellungen annähernd herzustellen ist, ist die Lichtregie im Autohaus immer ein Kompromiss, der sich aus den Erfordernissen der verschiedenen Funktionen und Funktionsbereiche ergibt. Konträre Anforderungen – hier geht es um Stimmung, da um Tageslicht-Simulation, dort um ergonomische Funktionsbeleuchtung – müssen sorgfältig gegeneinander abgewogen und miteinander harmonisiert werden.

Konkret heißt das, unterschiedliche „Lichtzonen" unauffällig voneinander zu trennen. Dies geschieht einerseits durch eine differenzierte Beleuchtungstechnik und entsprechende Leuchtkörper, andererseits durch Tageslichtsteuerung an den Fassaden, drittens durch ein entsprechendes Farb- bzw. Materialkonzept

large glass fronts does not easily allow for "controlled lighting". Depending on weather and sunlight, the windows reflect the environment on the outside of the building rather than allowing effective viewing into the interior exhibition spaces; the area around the window fronts – that is to say, the preferred exhibition space – is subject to an ever-changing mixture of directed daylight and diffused artificial light, which create an environment that is extremely difficult to control. The requirements of ambient interior lighting are met more often than optimised vehicle lighting.

All the same, the cars are still the "main actors" in the showroom; their presentation has priority. The vehicle contours must be demonstrated as elegantly and effectively as possible; varnished surfaces should shine and show hardly any light reflections. In addition, the area around the cars should be as free of blinding as possible, whereas the "atmospheric" light of the customer zone should not diminish the light effects on the vehicles themselves.

Contrary to the "black-box technique" that is often used at trade fairs and exhibitions, the lighting in a car showroom is always a compromise, resulting from the requirements of different functions and functional areas. In each individual case, opposite requirements – for example, atmosphere, daylight simulation or ergonomic functional lighting – have to be very carefully weighed up and harmonised.

Concretely, this means that different "light zones" should be separated discreetly. This is effected, firstly, through a differentiated lighting technique and corresponding lights; secondly, through the directing of daylight at the façades; and thirdly through an appropriate colour and materials concept both inside and outside of the building, which supports the creation of functional zones through lighting. The lighting will create a dramatic effect through alternating "cold " and "warm" spaces with corresponding colours, the result being that the different areas address the customers in either a neutral or an emotional way.

Pastellfarben und warmes Licht dominieren in den Verweil- und Wartezonen des Autohauses.

Pastel colours and warm light dominate in the resting and waiting zones of the showroom.

Gastlichkeit braucht Atmosphäre: der Bistro-Bereich

Hospitality needs atmosphere: the bistro area.

im und am Gebäude, welches die lichttechnische Zonierung des Autohauses in verschiedene Funktionsbereiche unterstützt. In der Dramaturgie des Lichtdesigns läuft das auf eine Abfolge von „kalten" bzw. „warmen" Beleuchtungssphären (mit den jeweiligen Farbkonzepten) hinaus. Räumlich entsprechen ihnen Bereiche, in denen es auf der einen Seite um eine sachliche, auf der anderen um eine emotionale Kundenansprache geht.

Differenziert eingesetzte Deckenlichtsysteme schaffen die Grundbeleuchtung im Autohaus. In den primären Kundenkontaktzonen – der Info-Theke und Verkäuferplätzen – kommt es in erster Linie auf eine funktionsgerechte, ergonomische Beleuchtung der Arbeitsplätze an. Hier findet man Pendelleuchten, breit strahlende Arbeitslampen und an der Theke eine verdeckte, d.h. für den Kunden nicht sichtbare Arbeitsplatzbeleuchtung. Die Wand- und Materialfarben in dieser Zone sind kühl: blau, grau, silbern und verschiedene Holztöne.

Eine sachliche Atmosphäre herrscht auch im Bereich der Kundendienstannahme. Sie ist gewissermaßen das Entrée zur Werkstatt. Parallel zum Fahrzeug bzw. den Hebebühnen verlaufende, entspiegelte Lichtbänder schaffen optimale, d.h. gleichmäßige Helligkeit.

Weitere Kundenkontaktzonen sind Bistro und Shop. Das Bistro dient der behaglichen Einstimmung, es ist ein Ort des Verweilens, auch Wartezone. Hier werden warme Farben (Apricot) und dezentes, warmes Licht eingesetzt. Designerleuchten und entsprechendes Mobiliar sorgen für eine stilvolle Atmosphäre – ähnlich wie im Merchandising-Bereich, der im Idealfall die Anmutung einer edlen Boutique hat. Vitrinen, Regale bzw. die dort ausgestellten Accessoires werden von Spots direkt angestrahlt und damit aus der Umgebung optisch hervorgehoben.

Im Ausstellungsbereich für die Fahrzeuge werden, wie schon angedeutet, ganz besondere Anforderungen an das Lichtkonzept gestellt, weil sich hier das natürliche Tageslicht und die installierte Lichttechnik vermischen. Die Exponatfläche ist zudem eine Bühne, die sich – zumindest bei den kleineren Autohaus-Formaten – dem Publikum bzw. den Kunden von zwei Seiten vorteilhaft darstellen können muss: den

Subtly differentiated integrated ceiling lights constitute the basic lighting in car showrooms. In the primary contact zones – such as the information and sales desks – functional, ergonomic lighting of the workstations has utmost priority; this includes the use of pendant lamps, wide-angle desk lamps and covered workstation lighting at the counter, all of which is invisible to the customer. The wall and material colours in this zone are cool, comprising blue, grey, and silver and various wood tones.

The customer service reception also maintains a neutral atmosphere. It is, so to speak, a form of an entrance to the workshop. Parallel to the vehicles or ramps run coated lighting strips, which create an optimised, even brightness.

Other client contact zones include the bistro and the shop. In the bistro visitors can become acclimatised. It is an area where clients can linger and relax, and it also serves as a kind of waiting room. Warm colours (apricot) and discreet, warm lights are used here; designer lamps and furniture create a stylish environment – similar to that of the merchandising area, which should ideally resemble an up-market boutique. Display cases, shelves and the exhibited accessories are directly lit by spotlights and optically highlighted, that is set off from their environment.

As previously described, the car exhibition area has special lighting requirements, because natural daylight and the installed light technology are mixed together. Especially in the case of small showrooms, the exhibition surface also represents a stage, which has to present itself positively from two sides to customers and the audience, to the people passing by outside and to the visitors inside the building.

In principle, the lighting in the exhibition zone has to be able to react flexibly to the changes of daytime and sunlight, in order for the depth of the space to be visible in all weather conditions. Large adjustable light sails above the vehicles are used in particular for this purpose.

Passanten im Außenraum sowie den Besuchern im Innern des Gebäudes.

Prinzipiell muss die Lichttechnik in der Ausstellungszone auf den Wechsel der Tageszeiten und der Sonneneinstrahlung flexibel reagieren können, und zwar so, dass die Tiefe dieses Funktionsbereichs möglichst unter allen Wetterbedingungen auch von außen wahrnehmbar bleibt. Dafür sorgen insbesondere große, in der Beleuchtungsstärke regelbare Lichtsegel über den Fahrzeugen.

Die Lichtfarbe und -temperatur der Lichtquellen simuliert hier Tageslicht. Es muss vermieden werden, dass „falsche" Farbwirkungen und lästige Reflexe entstehen; dies wird durch die Technik, durch große Lichtpunkthöhen und durch entsprechend eingesetzte Wandschirme erreicht, welche die aus dem Innern des Gebäudes eindringende „Lichtsauce" kompensieren bzw. ausschalten.

Erst bei Nacht entsteht eine perfekt kontrollierbare Lichtsituation. Die Autohäuser nutzen dies, indem einzelne Bereiche fließend abgedunkelt werden, so dass der Blick der Passanten auf einige wenige, bewusst in Szene gesetzte „Highlights" der Fahrzeugparade hinter der Fassade gelenkt werden kann. Akzentuiert wird dieses Außenbild durch Mast- und Pollerleuchten und durch eine Hervorhebung des Eingangsbereichs.

Here, the light colour and temperature of the light source simulate daylight. Unwanted colour effects and reflections should be avoided through the use of technology, with high light point fixtures and through strategically positioned wall screens. These should successfully compensate or neutralise the "light cocktail" coming from the building's interior.

It is only at night that perfectly controllable lighting can be successfully achieved. Car showrooms take advantage of this opportunity to darken isolated areas, so that the attention of pedestrians can be directed to a few well-staged highlights of the vehicle parade behind the façade. This external image is accentuated by pole lights and bollard lamps, which highlight the entrance area.

Abends wird das Autohaus zur
optimal ausgeleuchteten
Vitrine: Beispiel aus Crailsheim

The showroom becomes an
optimally lit cabinet in the
evenings: an example from
Crailsheim.

In der Ausstellungszone des
Autohauses sorgen Lichtsegel
und Sonnenschutzblenden
an der Fassade für kontrollierbare Lichtverhältnisse (links);
im Bereich der Infotheken
dominieren gut gestaltete
Funktionsleuchten.

In the exhibition zones in the
showrooms light sails and sunshades on the façades ensure
monitored lighting conditions
(left); the designed functional
lighting dominates in the
Information points area.

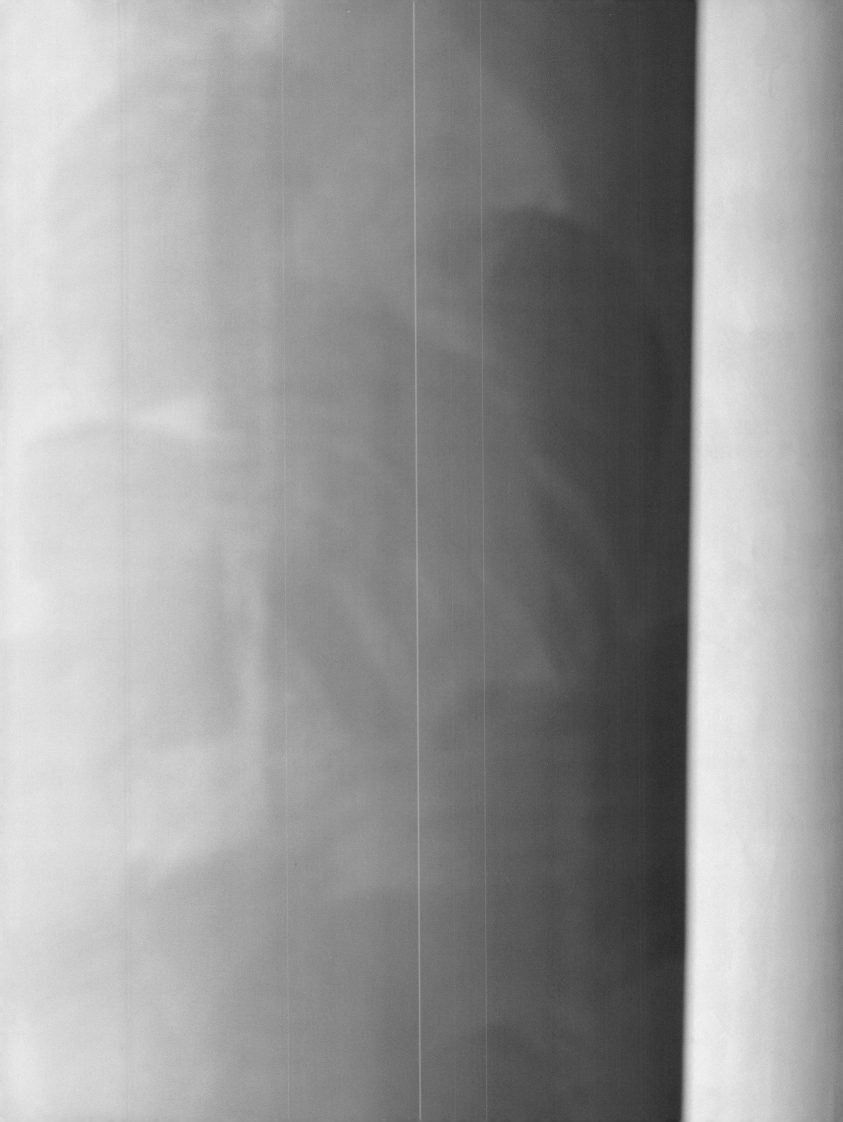

Wie in der Boutique: Inszenie-rung von Merchandising-Artikeln im Shop-Bereich

Just like in a boutique: stage-management of merchandising articles in the shop area.

Medieneinsatz für Vertrieb und Marke
Use of media in sales and brand

Fahrzeuginfo

Steigen Sie ein und erleben Sie die E Klasse Limousine.

Fahrzeuginformationssystem als interaktives, dialogisches Medium

Vehicle information system as an interactive dialogue medium

Medieneinsatz für Vertrieb und Marke

Use of media in sales and brand

Auf avancierte Medien gestütztes *Branding* – also etwa Zielgruppen- und Kundenkommunikation via Internet – ist fast schon eine Selbstverständlichkeit geworden. Woran noch eifrig gearbeitet wird, ist dagegen die enge Verknüpfung von Markenkommunikation, Erlebniskauf, Service und Beratung mit Hilfe interaktiver Medien.

Der gegenwärtig noch insulare Medieneinsatz bei der Inszenierung von Markenwelten wird in naher Zukunft von integrierten Konzepten abgelöst. Mit anderen Worten: Die gewohnte Unterscheidung (und subjektiv empfundene Rangfolge) von „authentischen" und „medialisierten" Markenerlebnissen wird in absehbarer Zeit obsolet sein – spätestens dann nämlich, wenn die Generation der Computerkids zur marktentscheidenden Käuferschicht herangewachsen ist.

Das Autohaus-Konzept von Mercedes-Benz trägt dieser Entwicklung schon jetzt Rechnung. Prototypen eines Kunden-Informationssystems, das modular aufgebaut und international einsetzbar ist, sind bereits im Einsatz. Sie dienen nicht nur dem *Branding*, sondern unterstützen gleichzeitig auch die Beratungs- und Verkaufsaktivitäten in den Marken-Niederlassungen. Mittelfristig werden die herkömmlich, d.h. mit vorhandenen oder überspielten AV-Konserven betriebenen Displays, Monitore und Flatscreens wohl ganz durch die Hard- und Software dieses interaktiven Systems ergänzt werden.

Sein „Baukasten"-Prinzip reflektiert die unterschiedlichen Ansprüche und Erwartungen, denen es in den jeweiligen Autohaus-Formaten zu genügen hat. Künftig soll es mit diesem Instrument möglich sein, auch auf kleinen Markenplattformen die gesamte Produktpalette von Mercedes-Benz in allen ihren Dimensionen und Ausprägungen virtuell präsent zu halten: Das Spektrum reicht vom emotional geprägten Produktfilm über die 3D-Visualisierung von Modell- und Ausstattungsvarianten bis hin zu fahrzeugspezifischen Infomercials über technische Features.

Die Einsatzmöglichkeiten der System-Terminals sind universal. Sie kommen an den „Themeninseln" der

Use of media in sales and brand

Branding supported by advanced media – meaning communication with target groups and customers via the Internet – has almost become the norm. The close linking up of brand communication, event shopping, service and consulting with the aid of interactive media is, however, still being worked on.

The present, still insular use of media in the staging of brand worlds will be replaced by integrated concepts in the near future. In other words: the usual differentiation (and subjective ranking order) of "authentic" and "mediarised" brand experiences will become obsolete in the foreseeable future – namely at the latest when this generation of computer kids has grown up to be the consumer group dominating the market.

The Mercedes-Benz car dealership concept has already taken this development into account. Prototypes of a customer information system, which is both modular and can be used internationally, is already being used. These prototypes do not only serve *branding*, but also at the same time support the consulting and sales activities in brand subsidiaries. In the mid-term conventional tools, that is, displays, monitors and flatscreens powered by the available or pre-recorded AV material, will be completely complemented by the hardware and software of this interactive system.

Its "building blocks" concept reflects the varying requirements and expectations which need to be satisfied in each of the car dealership formats. In the future this instrument should make it possible to keep the complete spectrum of products, in all their dimensions and with all their characteristics, in virtual form in the smaller brand platforms as well. This spectrum ranges from emotional product films to 3D visualisations of models and variations of furnishings. It also includes vehicle-specific infomercials on technical features and second-hand cars.

The application possibilities for these system terminals are universal. They can be used on the theme islands in the car dealerships just as well as in the lounge areas or in the workplaces occupied by consultants and sales reps. The content of the

Autohäuser ebenso zum Einsatz wie in den Lounge-Bereichen oder an den Arbeitsplätzen der Berater bzw. Verkäufer. Das Informationssystem ist inhaltlich so konfiguriert, dass es die erlebnisorientierte und gefühlsbetonte Markenkommunikation ebenso stützt wie den sachlich-informellen Dialog zwischen Vertrieb und Kundschaft – und dabei immer *up to date* ist.

So groß der qualitative Vorsprung des neuen, interaktiven Informationssystems gegenüber den herkömmlich genutzten Medien auch sein mag – die Integration der Endgeräte in das architektonische Ambiente der unterschiedlichen Autohausformate folgt denselben Prinzipien, die auch für die „alten" neuen Medien gelten.

Die transparente Architektur der Autohäuser, die Fülle des einfallenden Tageslichts und die Kaskaden des komplementär eingesetzten Kunstlichts setzen wesentlich die Rahmenbedingungen für den Medieneinsatz. Hier gilt es, auf die herrschenden Beleuchtungsverhältnisse Rücksicht zu nehmen – auf Gegenlicht, auf Bildschirmreflexe etc. Gegebenenfalls muss die Präsentationszone, in der die Medien eingesetzt werden, durch Wandschirme oder Sonnensegel präpariert werden.

Eine gestalterisch ansprechende, markenneutrale „Verpackung" der Medien und Endgeräte ist überall dort notwendig, wo sie als Elemente der Raum- und Markeninszenierung prägend sind oder sein können. In der Regel ist das in einem *Brand Center* der Fall, bei einer „Themeninsel" oder in der Lounge des Autohauses, seltener oder gar nicht an den Arbeitsplätzen der Verkäufer. Insbesondere das Pylon-Konzept für die interaktiven Systeme in den Mercedes-Benz Centern in München und Berlin dient als gestalterische Klammer für Medien und Architektur.

Hinsichtlich der Benutzer- und Wartungsfreundlichkeit, des inhaltlichen Spektrums und der Aktualisierungsrhythmen wird das dialogische Informationssystem permanent weiterzuentwickeln sein. In gewisser Hinsicht ist es ein - kundenseitiges - Komplement des digitalen „Markenstudios", das - als internes Planungsinstrument - im Kapitel *Die Marke in den Metropolen* beschrieben wird.

information system is configured in such a way that it supports brand communication, emphasising experience and emotions, as well as the exchange of factual information between the sales team and customers. It is thus always *up to date*.

However large the qualitative lead of the new interactive information system may be compared to conventional media, the integration of the end-devices into the architectonic ambience of the various showroom formats follows the same principles which are applied to the "old" new media.

The transparent architecture of the car dealerships, the amount of daylight shining into the building and the cascades of artificial light used additionally, are essential elements determining the tone for the use of media. One has to take into account the lighting conditions that dominate here – contre-jour light, screen reflections etc. In some cases the presentations zone, where the media will be used, has to be prepared using screens or awnings.

The "packaging" of media and end-devices with an attractive and brand-neutral design is necessary in all the places where they are, or might become, a characteristic element of the spatial environment and brand staging. This is mainly the case with the theme islands or in a *brand centre* or even in the lounge of a showroom; rarer or not at all at workplaces for the sales staff. In particular, the pylon concept for the interactive systems serves as a design link between the media and architecture in the Mercedes-Benz Centres in Munich and Berlin.

Regarding aspects such as user and maintenance friendliness, the range of content and the updating rhythms – the dialogue information system needs to be developed constantly. To a certain degree it is – a customers' – complement to the digital "brand studio", which is described as an internal planning instrument in the chapter *The brand in the metropolis*.

Besucherinformationssystem Visitor information system

Event-Marketing und Architektur
Event marketing and architecture

Die Marke als Gastgeber,
hier im Mercedes-Benz Center
München.

The brand as the host:
the Mercedes-Benz Centre
in Munich

Event-Marketing und Architektur

Event-Marketing und Architektur

Vermutlich die erste Beschreibung eines – noch fiktiven – Marketing-Events der Automobilindustrie stammt von dem architekturverliebten und zu skurrilen Ideen neigenden Schriftsteller Paul Scheerbart. Ende 1907 veröffentlichte er in dem Blatt *Morgen* eine Skizze, welche die Überschrift *Das Automobil-Theater* trägt und von einer Road Show erzählt. Es ist ein Text von geradezu prophetischer Qualität, deshalb sei er hier in voller Länge wiedergegeben:

„Die Automobilindustrie hat sich über einen Mangel an Käufern zu beklagen, und so lässt man sich auf kostspielige Experimente ein, um die Interessensphäre zu erweitern. Und so kam es, dass in der vorigen Woche von einer bekannten Automobilfabrik ein imposantes Schauspiel arrangiert wurde, zu dem die meisten Theaterpotentaten Norddeutschlands geladen waren. Es erschienen u. a. auch Brahm, Lindau, Reinhardt, Hauptmann, Zickel und Bonn. Durch einen Zufall kam es, dass ich auch dabei war. Es wurden zehn Lastautomobile vorgeführt, in denen sich alles, was zu einem Theaterbau notwendig ist, vorfand. Und das Theater wurde in unsrer Gegenwart in einer halben Stunde von zehn Arbeitern ‚aufgebaut‘. Unter den Materialien herrschte Linoleum und Segeltuch vor, von Wellblech und Eisen war wenig zu bemerken; das Ganze bekam durch farbige Hölzer einen sehr frischen modernen Charakter. Und der Zuschauerraum konnte 150 Personen aufnehmen. Es wurde auch eine Szene aus Lessings ‚Minna von Barnhelm‘ gespielt. Und nach der Vorstellung wurde das ganze Theater in ein Restaurant verwandelt mit Küche, Garderobe und Nebenzimmern. Diese Verwandlung nahm kaum 7 Minuten in Anspruch. Zum Schlusse wurde das Restaurant in derselben Zeit in ein kleines Hotel verwandelt, in dem das gesamte Theaterpersonal mit allen Bequemlichkeiten für die Nacht untergebracht werden konnte. Somit werden wir demnächst auch ‚fahrende‘ Theater haben. Und diesem wird, nach dem Vorgeführten zu urteilen, nichts Schmierenartiges anhaften. Leider darf der Name der Automobilfirma noch nicht genannt werden, da zwischen dem Erfinder und der Firma noch einige Differenzen bestehen, die erst beseitigt werden müssen. Es ist der Bau von zehn solchen Wandertheatern von der Firma beschlossen worden."

Event marketing and architecture

The first description of a fictional marketing event for the automobile industry probably dates back to the lover of architecture and eccentric author Paul Scheerbart. At the end of 1907, he published a draft entitled "The automobile theatre" in the paper "Morgen", where he mentions a road show. This text is quite prophetic and therefore we would like to reproduce it here in its entirety:

"The car industry suffers from a lack of buyers. Therefore a number of expensive experiments are being undertaken to expand its area of interest. That is why a well-known car manufacturer organised an impressive spectacle last week, to which most of the great names of the North-German theatre landscape were invited. Amongst those who attended were Brahm, Lindau, Reinhardt, Hauptmann, Zickel and Bonn. Coincidentally, I attended as well. The event involved ten trucks containing everything necessary for a theatre production. While we were there, the theatre was "erected" by ten workers within half an hour. The dominant materials were linoleum and sailcloth, not a trace of corrugated iron or iron; coloured wood gave the whole thing a fresh, modern character. The auditorium seated 150 people. A scene from Lessing's "Minna von Barnhelm" was performed. After the play, the whole theatre was transformed into a restaurant with kitchen, cloakroom and side-rooms. This transformation barely took seven minutes. At the end, the restaurant was transformed into a small, comfortable hotel, where the whole theatre crew was put up for the whole night. In the future, we will see more of these "mobile" theatres. And if we judge by what I have just described, they will not be shoddy. Unfortunately the name of the car firm cannot be disclosed yet, until a few differences between the inventor and the firm have been evened out. The company has decided to build ten such touring theatres."

Which scene from "Minna von Barnhelm" did Scheerbart have in mind when he mentioned the play in this context? Probably not a specific one, as even today brand events do not have a very

Welche Szene aus *Minna von Barnhelm* hatte Scheerbart wohl im Sinn, als er das Stück in diesem Kontext erwähnte? Vermutlich keine bestimmte, denn das Event-Marketing hat auch heute noch keine besonders zuverlässige Grundlage in der Theorie und Praxis des Markenmanagements. Es bewegt sich unstet zwischen dem Design jeweils „markenkonformer" Ereignisse, bei denen mitunter enorme Streuverluste einkalkuliert sind, und der scharf auf definierte Zielgruppen fokussierten Konzeption von Veranstaltungen, deren Verlauf dann allerdings nicht selten den entsprechenden Markenbezug vermissen lässt.

Event-Marketing hat ein breites Spektrum. Es gibt programmzentrierte Events, deren Fokus klar auf eine dramaturgisch strukturierte Darbietung ausgerichtet ist, und gäste- bzw. kundenzentrierte Events mit dialogischem Charakter, kleine und große Veranstaltungen. Geht es hier um dramaturgisch aufgeputztes Entertainment für gemischtes Publikum, organisiert man da informelle Begegnungen in kleinem Kreis. Manche Marketingstrategen bevorzugen Galas und Benefizveranstaltungen, andere wollen lieber den Kunden selbst etwas Gutes tun und bieten Vorträge zu Wirtschaftsthemen oder Modenschauen an.

In jedem Fall muss, wer *inhouse* Event-Marketing betreibt, die räumlichen und technischen Voraussetzungen schaffen, um solche Veranstaltungen korrekt und zielgerecht durchführen zu können. Es geht im Wesentlichen um

- Flächen für Podien und Gäste
- Bühnen- und Lichttechnik
- geeignete Bestuhlungssysteme
- Infrastruktur für Medien und Catering
- Ausstellungssysteme

Die Markenarchitektur von Mercedes-Benz bietet in allen Autohäusern die räumlichen Grundvoraussetzungen für „formatgerechte" Events. Explizit und bis in die Details zu planen ist allerdings nur die eventbezogene Infrastruktur der großen Autohäuser, insbesondere der Mercedes-Benz Center. Hier geht es um die optimierte Platzierung von Medienwänden, um freie Sichtbeziehungen zwischen Bühnen bzw. Podien und Auditorium, um die funktionale Zuordnung von Gastronomie und Küche, Material- und Stuhldepots etc.

solid theoretical or practical basis for their brand management. They range from events "in line with the brand", where extreme spread losses are factored in, to events focused on clearly defined target groups, which often miss a very transparent reference to the brand.

Event marketing is a wide field. The events are centred on a programme or on guests/clients; there are small or large events; there might be dramatically orchestrated entertainments for a mixed audience, or informal meetings for a small group; some marketing strategists prefer galas and charity events, others want to offer their clients immediate benefits and organise presentations on economical topics or fashion shows.

In any case, *in-house* event marketing requires the right spatial and technical conditions if events are to be implemented in a targeted and relevant way. The key components are

- surfaces for platforms and guests
- stage and light technology
- suitable seating facilities
- media and catering infrastructures
- exhibition systems

Mercedes-Benz's brand architecture makes sure that all its car showrooms offer the spatial prerequisites for "adequately formatted events". However, only the event-related infrastructure of bigger showrooms, such as the Mercedes-Benz Centre, needs explicit and detailed planning. What matters is the optimised location of media surfaces, free visual transitions between the stage or platform and the auditorium, and a functional, spatial division for catering and kitchen, material and chair storage, etc.

Big events with perfect service for up to 1,500 guests have to run smoothly, because they showcase the hospitality of the brand. It is here that customer loyalty can be impacted considerably in a negative or positive way.

Like all other brand incarnations, the content of these Mercedes-Benz events concentrates on brand values and the "attitude" of the brand.

Die Event-Tauglichkeit der
Architektur spielt vor allem
in den großen Autohaus-
formaten eine wichtige Rolle.

The architecture has to be
able to hold an event and this
plays an important role in
the large showroom formats.

Der Betrieb mit großem Publikum, der perfekte Service für bis zu 1.500 Gäste muss reibungslos vonstatten gehen können, denn bei Events zeigt sich die Marke als Gastgeber. Gerade in dieser Hinsicht kann in Sachen Kundenbindung viel gewonnen und viel verspielt werden.

Die inhaltlichen Aspekte von Events unter dem Mercedesstern orientieren sich – wie alle anderen Markenauftritte von Mercedes-Benz auch – an der Trias der Markenwerte und der „Haltung" der Marke.

In dieses Koordinatensystem müssen sich alle Veranstaltungskonzepte mitsamt ihrer Dramaturgie einordnen lassen: Es geht bei jedem Event darum, Engagement zu zeigen, Qualität zu bieten, Atmosphäre zu schaffen, den Zielgruppendialog auch und gerade dort ernst zu nehmen, wo es „nur" um Vergnügen, Unterhaltung und Lifestyle geht. Schließlich will und muss die Event-Kultur von Mercedes-Benz auch die eher abstrakten Dimensionen der „Orientierungswerte" bedienen, was zum Beispiel bedeuten kann, Veranstaltungen anzubieten, die wissens- und lernorientiert sind und geeignet, das Publikum in den Dialog etwa über gesellschaftliche Zukunftsfragen einzubeziehen.

Die Zielgruppenansprache der Marke Mercedes-Benz ist breit gefächert. Es gibt Programmkonzepte für Kinder und Jugendliche, für Kultur- und Sportinteressierte, für Technikfreaks, für Reiselustige und Modebegeisterte, für Abenteurer und Anleger, für Honoratioren in der Provinz und für Lebenskünstler in den Metropolen.

Die Evidenz des Markenbezugs einer Veranstaltung lässt sich dabei jeweils nur schwer messen. Event-Strategen brauchen deshalb einen langen Atem und viel Fingerspitzengefühl für das jeweilige Umfeld, in dem ein Event platziert wird. Das wichtigste Kriterium für die Qualität einer Veranstaltung hat schon Paul Scheerbart ex negativo benannt: ihr darf vor allem nichts „Schmierenartiges" anhaften.

All events and their orchestration must fit into this system: the objective is to show commitment and quality, create an atmosphere and take the dialogue with the target group seriously even in a context of fun, entertainment and lifestyle. The event culture of Mercedes-Benz also wants to, and must, serve the abstract dimensions of "orientation values". This means, for instance, offering events which are educational and knowledge-based and capable of involving the audience in a dialogue about future social questions.

The Mercedes-Benz brand tries to reach its target groups in many different ways. There are programmes for children and youth, for people interested in culture or sports, for fans of technology, people passionate about travel or fashion, for adventurers or investors, for notabilities in the provinces and connoisseurs in the metropolitan areas.

It is always difficult to measure how related the event is to the brand. Event strategists need perseverance and subtlety for each environment that hosts an event. An event's most important quality criteria was already known to Paul Scheerbart: there should not be anything shoddy about it.

**Events in der Passage:
Mercedes-Welt am Salzufer
in Berlin**

Events in the passageway:
Mercedes-Welt at the Salzufer
in Berlin

Zeichen aus Glas: Die ersten Mercedes-Benz
Center in Berlin und München
Glass symbols: the first Mercedes-Benz Centres
in Berlin and Munich

**Alter Standort, neues Haus: das
Mercedes-Benz Center in Berlin**

Old location, new building: the
Mercedes-Benz Centre in Berlin

Zeichen aus Glas: Die ersten Mercedes-Benz Center in Berlin und München

Zeichen aus Glas: Die ersten Mercedes-Benz Center in Berlin und München

Die ersten Mercedes-Benz Center wurden in den Jahren 2000 und 2003 in Berlin bzw. in München eröffnet – jeweils an zentralen innerstädtischen Standorten, die schon seit Jahrzehnten eingeführte Mercedes-Benz Adressen sind. Konzeptionell und planerisch sind die Häuser in Berlin und München allerdings Produkte einer Übergangsphase, in der die Überlegungen zur künftigen Markenarchitektur von Mercedes-Benz, zur erlebnisorientierten Marken-darstellung und zu den neuen Retail-Formaten noch nicht bis ins Detail ausgearbeitet waren. Sie fügen sich folglich nur partiell der funktionalen und architektonischen Systematik, wie sie in den Eingangs-kapiteln beschrieben wurde.

Was sich in Berlin und München äußerlich und prima vista als gewissermaßen autonomer (weil noch nicht am System-Design der Mercedes-Benz Autohäuser orientierter) Architekturentwurf darstellt, wird bei näherem Hinsehen gleichwohl als Markenarchitektur erkennbar – als Architektur für die Marke Mercedes-Benz. Denn beide Bauten transportieren und kommu-nizieren auf ihre Weise und in individueller Ausprä-gung den Wertekanon der Marke.

Der Unterschied zum Konzept der neu projektierten Marken Center gründet nicht in einem Defizit an markentypischer Identität, sondern in der Abwesen-heit eines „Markenkerns": Man findet in Berlin und München noch keine architektonisch ausdifferen-zierten *Brand Galleries*.

Beiden Entwürfen gemeinsam ist der Ansatz, transparente Architektur zu schaffen: Das Berliner Mercedes-Benz Autohaus liegt wie ein gläserner Flugzeugträger am Salzufer. Das in München steht als kompakte Großskulptur wie ein schimmernder Fels im brandenden Autoverkehr – am Schnittpunkt von Arnulfstraße und Donnersberger Brücke im westlichen Stadtteil Neuhausen.

In Berlin wurde das neue Haus an traditionsreicher Adresse gebaut, nämlich am Salzufer, wo die Firma Benz & Cie bereits 1916 eine der größten

Glass symbols: the first Mercedes-Benz Centres in Berlin and Munich

The first Mercedes-Benz Centres were opened in 2000 and 2003 in Berlin and Munich at central addresses which had been established for decades. However, from a conceptual and planning point of view, the buildings in Berlin and Munich are part of a transitional period, where the new event-orientated brand architecture and retail formats have not yet been clearly formulated. They only partially fit into the new functional and architec-tural system described in the first chapters.

At first sight, the architecture in Berlin and Munich has a more autonomous appearance (as it does not yet follow the new system design of the Mercedes-Benz showrooms). However, it is still recognisable as Mercedes-Benz brand architecture. Both buildings communicate the brand value with different expressions and individual characteristics.

The difference with the concept of the new brand centre is not the lack of brand identity, but rather the absence of the "brand core". Architecturally differentiated Brand Galleries do not exist as yet in Berlin and Munich.

A common aspect of the architecture of both buildings is the attempt to create a sense of transparency. The Berlin centre, at the Salzufer, resembles a glass aircraft-carrier. The Munich building, at the intersection of Arnulfstraße and Donnersberger Brücke in the western city district of Neuhausen, has the appearance of a compact sculpture, standing like a glistening rock in the thunderous traffic.

In Berlin, the new building is located at a tradi-tional address, at the Salzufer, where the company Benz & Cie erected one of the biggest repair workshops in 1916. Ever since its merger with the Daimler-Motorengesellschaft in the mid-twenties, the company's head office has remained situated at this location, at the Landwehrkanal, not far from the Straße des 17. Juni (Berlin's big East–West axis).

Reparaturwerkstätten errichtet hatte. Seit der Fusion der Firma mit der Daimler-Motorengesellschaft Mitte der zwanziger Jahre diente dieser Industriestandort am Landwehrkanal unweit der Straße des 17. Juni (der großen Ost-West-Achse Berlins) ununterbrochen als Hauptniederlassung des Unternehmens.

Das Umfeld des Berliner Mercedes-Benz Centers zwischen dem nahen S-Bahnhof Tiergarten, dem Landwehrkanal und der nördlich verlaufenden Spree soll gemäß dem „Planwerk Innenstadt" der Berliner Senatsverwaltung zur „Spreestadt Charlottenburg" weiterentwickelt werden – ein Urbanisierungsprozess, der gegenwärtig noch in seinen Anfängen steckt. Die Nachbarschaft der Mercedes-Welt besteht im Wesentlichen aus Bauten des frühen zwanzigsten Jahrhunderts – der ehemaligen Zwietusch-Fabrik des Siemens-Architekten Hans Hertlein aus den 20er-Jahren und dem in den 30er-Jahren gebauten Ernst-Reuter-Haus an der Straße des 17. Juni. Hier setzt das von den Stuttgarter Architekten Lamm-Weber-Donath und Partner geplante Mercedes-Benz Center den vorläufig ersten zeitgenössischen Akzent in Architektur und Städtebau.

„Thema" des etwa 160 Meter langen, der gestreckten Kurve des Landwehrkanals folgenden Gebäudes ist die Passage. Diese verläuft ungefähr in Ost-West-Richtung, ist etwa 15 Meter breit und bildet den luftigen Kern einer Spirale aus gemächlich ansteigenden Rampen und umlaufenden Galerien, auf der die gesamte Produktpalette der Mercedes-Benz Pkws in eindrucksvoller Variationsbreite ausgestellt ist. Ordnung und Übersicht schaffen „Themeninseln", die einzelne Baureihen in unterschiedlicher Ausstattung gruppenweise präsentieren bzw. Platz für Sonderausstellungen und -programme bieten. Dazu gehören etwa die Kinderfahrschule, der Formel-1-Rennsimulator oder eine Oldtimer-Ausstellung.

Die Architektur des Hauses und seine kommunikative Offenheit kommen dem Betreiberkonzept sehr entgegen: Im Berliner Mercedes-Benz Center haben Events einen hohen Stellenwert. Autohaus, Markenwelt und Veranstaltungsprogramm gehen zwanglos ineinander über. Die Dramaturgie ist nicht allein auf die engere Mercedes-Benz Klientel ausgerichtet, sondern in

Following recent urbanisation plans of the Berlin senate, the area around the Berlin Mercedes-Benz Centre will be developed into "Spreestadt Charlottenburg". The district in question lies between the Tiergarten train station, the Landwehrkanal and the river Spree running north. This process of urbanisation is currently still in its early stages. The buildings in the area date from the early 20th century: the former Zwietusch factory by Siemens architect Hans Hertlein was built in the twenties and the Ernst-Reuter-Haus, on the Straße des 17.Juni, in the thirties. The planned Mercedes-Benz Centre by Stuttgart architects Lamm-Weber-Donath and Partner will be the first milestone of contemporary architecture.

The "theme" of the approximately 160-meter-long building is a corridor, which follows the long drawn-out curve of the Landwehrkanal. It follows an east–west orientation, is about 15 metres wide and forms the core of a stretched spiral of ramps and surrounding galleries. The entire Mercedes product range is exhibited in its impressive diversity. It contains clearly structured and well-ordered themed islands, grouping the different car series and trims, and provides space for special exhibitions and programmes. Examples include the children's driving school, the formula 1 race simulator and a vintage car exhibition.

The communicative and open architecture of the building fits in with the focus on the sales concept. At the Berlin Mercedes-Benz Centre events have high priority. Showroom, brand world and events programmes are combined seamlessly. Not only are Mercedes customers targeted, but also potential clients and more remote target groups.

It therefore goes without saying that the infrastructure of the building is perfectly geared towards the events concept. There are efficient catering facilities in the passageway, a services "marketplace", an LED-screen for presenting films and television programmes to large audiences, an oval conference room and climbing walls in the action area. And, of course, in this dynamically curved car cathedral there is enough space to seat

Das Dampfermotiv in der
Markenarchitektur: der gläserne Bug des Hauses am Salzufer
in Berlin

The steamer motif in brand
architecture: the glass bow
of the building at the Salzufer
in Berlin

besonderem Maß auch auf potentielle Kunden und fernere Zielgruppen.

Es versteht sich, dass die Infrastruktur des Hauses perfekt auf die Anforderungen des Event-Konzepts ausgerichtet ist. Es gibt eine leistungsfähige Gastronomie in der Passage, einen „Marktplatz" für Service-Angebote, eine große LED-Wand zur Präsentation von Filmen und Fernsehprogrammen vor großem Publikum, einen in den „Bug" des Hauses eingehängten, ovalen Tagungsraum, Kletterwände als *Action Area*, und natürlich bietet diese dynamisch geschwungene Auto-Kathedrale hinreichend Platz für Besucher (2000) und temporäre Bühnenaufbauten. Dabei sorgt die intelligente räumliche Organisation des Hauses dafür, dass der Event-Betrieb nie mit dem Werkstattservice (rund um die Uhr im 3-Schicht-Betrieb) in Konflikt gerät.

Das Münchner Mercedes-Benz Center, entworfen und gebaut vom Münchner Büro LAI Lanz Architekten und Generalplaner, verkörpert trotz mancher Parallelen eine andere Philosophie. Auch hier handelt es sich um eine eingeführte „Adresse". Die zuvor über eine Fläche von 65.000 Quadratmetern verteilten Funktionen wurden allerdings beim Neubau auf einem Drittel der Grundstücksfläche in einer geschlossenen Gebäudeform untergebracht.

Das äußere Erscheinungsbild der Architektur appelliert nicht an den Flaneur, sondern an den Autofahrer, der sich auf Ausfall- und Ringstraßen schnell vorbeibewegt. Ein ovaler gläserner Turm fungiert als urbanes Stadtzeichen. Er beherrscht am Schnittpunkt der Verkehrsachsen einen voluminösen, fünfstöckigen und annähernd rechteckigen Kubus, der ebenfalls mit Glas verkleidet ist.

Die Architektur wirkt wie eine minimalistische Skulptur – sehr robust trotz der gläsernen Fassaden. Transparenz ist nicht das einzige architektonische Thema des Hauses, dominant ist die geschlossene, zeichenhafte Form. Ob die gläserne Hülle sich dem außerhalb des Gebäudes stehenden (oder fahrenden) Betrachter als spiegelnde Oberfläche oder als Diaphanbild präsentiert, hängt von der Witterung, dem Lichteinfall und natürlich von den Tageszeiten ab.

2,000 visitors and install temporary stage sets. The intelligent space division ensures that events do not conflict with the repair service (around the clock, in three shifts).

The Munich Mercedes-Benz Centre, designed and built by the Munich architects LAI Lanz Architekten und Generalplaner, follows another philosophy, despite other some other parallels. It is also located at an established address. Whereas previously the different functions were spread across 65,000 square metres, the new building occupies only a third of that surface in one compact structure.

The appearance of the external architecture is not so much directed at strollers as at car drivers going past the building on arterial and ring roads. At the intersection of the traffic arteries, a dominating oval glass tower forms an urban landmark; it takes the shape of a voluminous, five-storey glass-clad cube.

The architecture appears to be a minimalist sculpture that is very robust despite its glass facades. Transparency is not the only architectural theme of the building; it is its closed, iconic shape that is dominating. The weather, light conditions and, of course, the time of day, determine whether the glass shell appears as a reflective surface or as a transparent image.

In the early evening light, the illuminated casket shows off its treasures in all their splendour and becomes one big showcase. The main facades of the building are constructed "glass shelves" providing ample space for the exhibited cars. The art inside the building uses light as its most important design motif. The Stuttgart-born artists Andreas Schmid and Pietro Sanguineti, now working in Berlin, have created discreetly changing light sculptures at the lift tower (Schmid) and light boxes in the exhibition area (Sanguineti), supporting the aesthetical concept of the glass architecture and the "motion" and "technology" themes exhibited here.

Whereas the glass tower contains mostly offices, the main building hosting the actual client centre

Legendäre Oldtimer leisten
ihren Beitrag zur Inszenierung
aktueller Mercedes-Baureihen.

Legendary old-timers contri-
bute to the stage-management
of the Mercedes series today.

**Voller Setzkasten:
das Mercedes-Benz Center
in München**

Full shelves:
the Mercedes-Benz Centre
in Munich

Zeichen aus Glas: Die ersten Mercedes-Benz Center in Berlin und München

Bei anbrechender Dunkelheit zeigt die illuminierte Schatulle ihre Kostbarkeiten in besonderer Deutlichkeit und wird zum großen Schaufenster. Die Hauptfassaden des Gebäudes sind als „gläserne Regale" konstruiert, in deren Fächern die Fahrzeuge bequem Platz haben. Licht als Gestaltungsmittel ist übrigens auch das wichtigste Motiv der im Haus installierten Kunst: Die in Stuttgart geborenen und in Berlin tätigen Künstler Andreas Schmid und Pietro Sanguineti kommentieren mit einer changierenden Lichtskulptur am Aufzugsturm (Schmid) und Lichtkästen im Ausstellungsbereich (Sanguineti) auf diskrete Weise sowohl das ästhetische Konzept der Glasarchitektur wie auch die hier ausgestellten Themen „Bewegung" und „Technik".

Das Innere des Sockelgebäudes – es ist das eigentliche Kundenzentrum, im doppelschalig verglasten Turm sind überwiegend Büros untergebracht – zeigt im Kontrast zur offenen Struktur des Berliner Mercedes-Benz Centers eine sehr viel rigorosere Gliederung. Hinter der Front an der Arnulfstraße öffnet sich eine große, glasgedeckte Halle mit eingestellten Plateaus, die in der Regel der Präsentation von Fahrzeugen dienen, bei Bedarf aber auch als Bühnen zu nutzen sind. Von hier aus gelangt man über (Roll-)Treppen zu den drei Ausstellungsebenen im mittleren Gebäudeabschnitt. Dieser wird durch ein glasüberdachtes Atrium mit Tageslicht versorgt.

Das Konzept der „Themeninseln", das in Berlin seine Premiere hatte, prägt auch den Ausstellungsbetrieb in München. Die Präsentation von Neu- und Gebrauchtwagen erfolgt – anders als in Berlin – auf verschiedenen Ebenen, aber ebenfalls unter einem Dach. Während die Architektur des Berliner Hauses eine lineare Ausstellungsdramaturgie und die Inszenierung von Höhepunkten am (oberen) Ende der Promenade fast erzwingt, bieten sowohl die räumliche Organisation der Münchner Niederlassung wie auch deren leichter zu kontrollierende Lichtsituation ein breites Spektrum an Möglichkeiten der szenischen Inszenierung und Hierarchisierung der Exponate. Den hochwertigsten, spektakulärsten und neuesten Fahrzeugmodellen begegnet der Besucher in der Regel in der Halle und im ersten Obergeschoss, die oberste Ebene ist den Gebrauchtwagen vorbehalten.

has a much more rigorous structure than the Berlin Mercedes-Benz Centre. The front overlooking the Arnulfstrasse hides a big, glass-covered hall with plateaus, which are mainly used to present cars but can also serve as stages according to the occasion. From here, escalators lead to the three exhibition areas in the middle section of the building, which receives daylight through a glass-covered atrium.

The concept of "theme islands", which made its debut in Berlin, is also used in the exhibition space in Munich. Compared to Berlin, however, new and used cars are presented on different levels, but still under one roof. The Berlin building dictates a linear exhibition flow and its highlights need to be placed at the upper end of the promenade. The space and light conditions of the Munich building offer a wider range of possibilities for orchestrating exhibitions and presenting the exhibits hierarchically. In general, the newer, most valuable and more spectacular models are displayed in the hall and on the first floor, whereas the upper level is reserved for used cars.

The events concept in Munich differs in several points from that of the Mercedes-Benz Centre in Berlin. Urbanity in Munich takes on a very different meaning to that in Berlin. The cities have very different characters and spatial conditions. In the open structure of the Berlin building, all visitors intentionally become part of the audience of events taking place in the corridor. The Munich architecture, however, makes it easier to hold events separately from the hustle and bustle of the exhibition area.

Does the characteristic architectural individualism of the Mercedes-Benz Centres in Berlin and Munich even slightly contradict the concept of homogenous brand architecture, which is to be recognised worldwide? The management of both Mercedes-Benz Centres is on the whole very satisfied with the strong architectural presence of their buildings in their respective urban contexts. At the same time, however, it supports the need for a worldwide design concept for its retail

Das Event-Konzept des Münchner Hauses unterscheidet sich in einigen Facetten von dem des Mercedes-Benz Centers Berlin. Urbanität heißt in München etwas anderes als in Berlin; und so spielt der individuelle Charakter des jeweiligen *Genius Loci* eine große Rolle, aber auch die räumlichen Bedingungen. In der offenen Struktur des Berliner Hauses sind praktisch alle Besucher immer auch Publikum eines in der Passage stattfindenden Events. In München ist es aufgrund der architektonischen Gegebenheiten leichter möglich, Veranstaltungen weitgehend separat vom Betrieb der Fahrzeugausstellung durchzuführen.

Steht die ausgeprägte architektonische Individualität der Mercedes-Benz Center in Berlin und München in einem – vielleicht auch nur leisen – Widerspruch zum Grundgedanken einer mit identischen Architekturdetails operierenden Gestaltungsstrategie, deren Ziel eine weltweit wiedererkennbare Markenarchitektur ist? Die Leitung beider Mercedes-Benz Center ist mit der starken architektonischen Präsenz ihrer Häuser in ihrem jeweiligen städtischen Umfeld sehr zufrieden. Sie geht aber gleichzeitig konform mit dem Anspruch, die Retail-Architektur von Mercedes-Benz weltweit nach klaren Vorgaben zu gestalten, sofern nur genügend Spielraum für regionale oder lokale Differenzierungsstrategien bleibt.

Tatsächlich relativiert sich im Falle der seit Jahrzehnten in Berlin und München tätigen Niederlassungen die Notwendigkeit, die Häuser unter Markengesichtspunkten regelgerecht „wiedererkennbar" zu gestalten; denn Marke und Unternehmen sind an den jeweiligen innerstädtischen Standorten bestens verwurzelt. Deshalb mag sich die Frage nach der Markenpräsenz im Stadtbild von Berlin und München auch anders stellen als, zum Beispiel, in überseeischen Märkten. Der Wettbewerb um Aufmerksamkeit vollzieht sich, soweit er mit architektonischen Mitteln ausgetragen wird, für deutsche Traditionsmarken in deutschen Märkten nicht allein nach den Regeln des Marken-Signalements.

Von Fall zu Fall ergibt sich deshalb vielleicht die Notwendigkeit, „Architekturpolitik" auch nach Maßgabe des jeweiligen *Genius Loci* zu machen: soweit absehbar ist, dass der Erfolg die Mittel heiligt – und sichergestellt ist, dass Ausnahmen die Regeln bestätigen.

architecture – as long as there is enough leeway, that is, for any regional and local differences.

In actual fact, since the Berlin and Munich branch offices have been established for decades, it is less crucial to make them recognisable. This is because brand and company are well rooted in their respective urban environments. The brand presence in cities overseas, as opposed to here in Berlin and Munich, has to be addressed differently. In the competition for consumer attention, in as far as this is to be achieved through architecture, German brands competing in traditional German markets do not solely operate according to rules of brand recognition.

In certain cases, it might well be recommendable to allow the local character to determine the individual architectural policy, as long as success justifies the means and these remain exceptions to the rule.

München leuchtet: der Büroturm des Mercedes-Benz Centers

Munich is lit: the office towers in the Mercedes-Benz Centre.

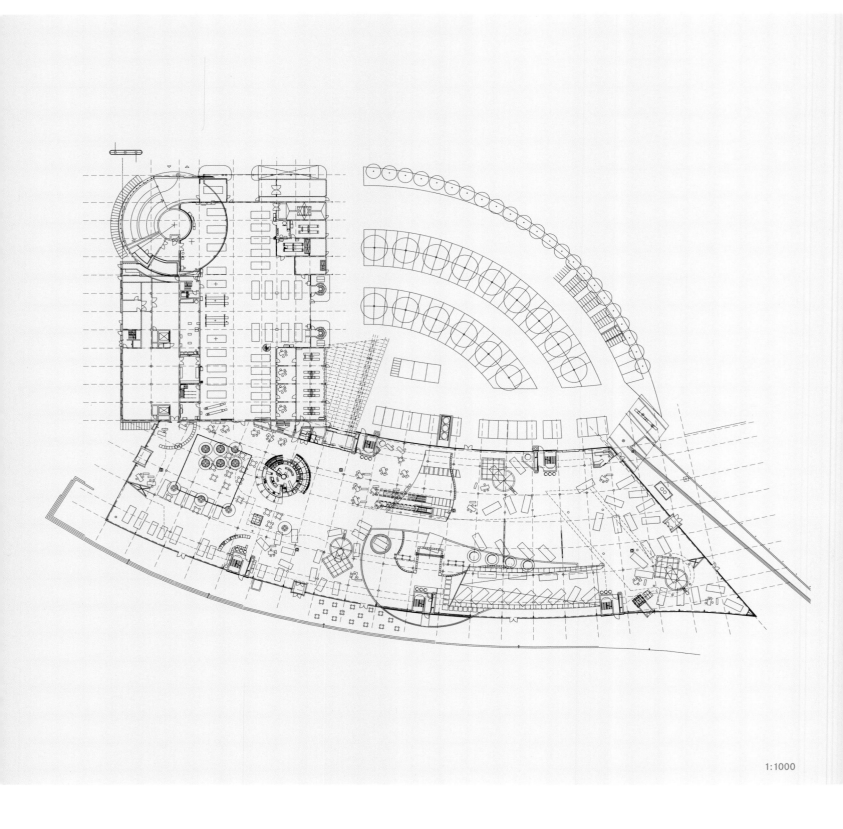

1:1000

Zeichen aus Glas: Die ersten Mercedes-Benz Center in Berlin und München

Initiale eines neuen Stadtteils, gespiegelt im Wasser des Landwehrkanals: Die Architektur des Berliner Mercedes-Benz Centers setzt den ersten zeitgenössischen Akzent in der geplanten „Spreestadt Charlottenburg". Links die Grundrissdarstellung des Erdgeschosses

Initials of a new district reflected in the water of the Landwehrkanal: The architecture of the Berlin Mercedes-Benz Centre introduces the first contemporary elements in the planned "Spreestadt Charlottenburg". Left an illustration of the plan of the ground floor.

Viele „Gesichter" hat der Baukörper des Berliner Autohauses:
Ansichten der Uferpromenade

The building of the Berlin showroom has many "faces": views of
the promenade at the shoreline.

Zeichen aus Glas: Die ersten Mercedes-Benz Center in Berlin und München

Großzügigkeit und Durch-
lässigkeit charakterisieren
das Raumkonzept des Hauses.
Zentrales Thema ist die ge-
krümmte Passage (rechts). Der
Konferenzraum ist in drama-
tischer Geste in den „Bug" der
Glasarchitektur eingestellt.

Spaciousness and permeability
characterise the spatial
concept of the building. The
central theme is the crooked
passage (right). The conference
room is set in a dramatic
gesture in the "bow" of the
glass architecture.

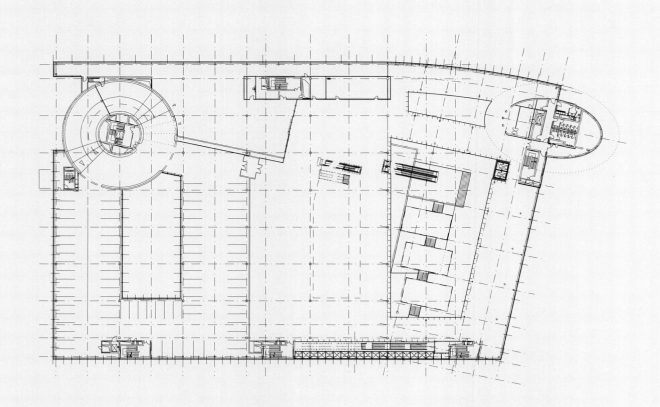

Zeichen aus Glas: Die ersten Mercedes-Benz Center in Berlin und München

Die Frontseite des Münchner Mercedes-Benz Centers an der Arnulfstraße; links die Darstellung des Grundrisses im Erdgeschoss.

The front of the Munich Mercedes-Benz Centre showroom in Arnulfstrasse: left an illustration of the plan of the ground floor.

Architektur für den bewegten Betrachter: Das Mercedes-Benz Center in München, gesehen von der Donnersberger Brücke.

Architecture for moved observers: the Mercedes-Benz Centre in Munich, seen from the Donnersberg bridge.

Zeichen aus Glas: Die ersten Mercedes-Benz Center in Berlin und München

Zeichen aus Glas: Die ersten Mercedes-Benz Center in Berlin und München

Zeichen aus Glas: Die ersten Mercedes-Benz Center in Berlin und München

Autohäuser stehen am besten
an Hauptverkehrsadern; Blick
über die Dächer Münchens

Showrooms are best located
at main traffic points: a view
of the roofs of Munich.

Bistro- und Ausstellungszone im Münchner Mercedes-Benz Center

Bistro and exhibition zones in the Munich Mercedes-Benz Centre.

Zeichen aus Glas: Die ersten Mercedes-Benz Center in Berlin und München

Blick hinter die Setzkastenfas-
sade (links) und in die Gastro-
nomiezone des Mercedes-Benz
Centers München.

View behind the case façade
(left) and of the gastronomy
zone of the Mercedes-Benz
Centre in Munich.

Die Marke in den Metropolen:
Mercedes-Benz Center der Zukunft
The brand in the metropolis:
Mercedes-Benz Centres of the future

Hier schlägt das Herz der
Marke: Modell des Mercedes-
Benz Centers in Stuttgart-
Untertürkheim; links im Hinter-
grund die Spindel des neuen
Mercedes-Benz Museums von
Ben van Berkel.

The heart of the brand beats
here: model of the Mercedes-
Benz Centre in Stuttgart-
Untertürkheim; left in back-
ground the spindle of the new
Mercedes-Benz Museum by
Ben van Berkel.

Die Marke in den Metropolen: Mercedes-Benz Center der Zukunft

Die Marke in den Metropolen:
Mercedes-Benz Center der Zukunft

Die geplanten und in naher Zukunft (2005 bis 2006) realisierten Mercedes-Benz Center in bedeutenden europäischen Städten wie etwa London, Mailand, Köln und Paris sind Großprojekte. In den Schlüsseldetails entsprechen sie den geschilderten Standards des architektonischen Konzepts. Ihre gewaltige Kubatur (durchschnittlich 120.000 Kubikmeter) und die großen Ausstellungsflächen machen es aber notwendig, die Gebäude einerseits städtebaulich sehr sorgfältig in ihr jeweiliges urbanes Umfeld einzufügen, andererseits die Fassaden differenziert zu gestalten und schließlich die Gebäudemassen selbst nutzungs- und vor allem kundenfreundlich zu organisieren.

Charakteristisch für alle in der Planung befindlichen Projekte ist der „Quartiergedanke": Ein Mercedes-Benz Center besteht aus vier bis fünf Gebäudeteilen, die in der Regel von der „Markengalerie" aus erschlossen werden. Die ausdifferenzierten Gebäudeteile sind gewissermaßen ein architektonisches Abbild der unterschiedlichen Fahrzeugklassen, die hier auf getrennten „Marktplätzen" präsentiert und thematisch inszeniert werden.

Die konischen Türme der Markengalerien setzen jeweils identische städtebauliche Akzente und tragen auf diese Weise zur Wiedererkennbarkeit des Markenauftritts bei. Das Prinzip des „gläsernen" Autohauses, das die kleineren Vertriebsformate wesentlich prägt, lässt sich bei den großen Mercedes-Benz Centern allerdings nicht durchhalten: Hier strukturieren große Wandscheiben und mit Kommunikationsmedien bestückte Flächen die Fassaden und sorgen gleichzeitig für eine kontrollierte bzw. kontrollierbare Lichtsituation im Gebäudeinnern.

Die Größe dieser Bauvorhaben stellt vor dem Hintergrund ihrer Funktion grundsätzlich ein ernstes Kommunikationsproblem dar: Wer die Architekturdebatten der letzten Jahrzehnte einigermaßen aufmerksam verfolgt hat, wird sich vergegenwärtigen, dass die komplexen Entstehungsbedingungen moderner architektonischer und städtebaulicher Großprojekte nicht nur die tradierten Rollen von Architekten, Planern,

The brand in the metropolis:
Mercedes-Benz Centres of the future

The Mercedes-Benz Centres that have been planned and will be realised in the near future (2005 to 2006) in significant European cities such as London, Milan, Cologne and Paris are large projects. As far as their key details are concerned they correspond to the standards outlined in the architectural concept; however, their tremendous cubature (average 120,000 cubic metres) and their large exhibition surfaces make it necessary, on the one hand, to very carefully adapt the building to the respective urban surroundings in consistency with urban developments, and on the other hand to design the façades in a differentiated way. Finally it is imperative to organise the building area in a user-friendly and, above all, customerfriendly manner.

A common characteristic of all the planned projects is the idea of quartering: A Mercedes-Benz Centre consists of four to five building segments which are, as a rule, accessible from the Brand Gallery. To an extent, the distinguishable building segments are an architectonic reflection of the varying classes of vehicles, which are displayed here on separated "market squares" and stage-managed thematically.

The Brand Galleries' conical towers emphasise the relevant identical urban development and are a contributing factor in the recognition value of the brand appearance. The principle of "glass" car dealerships, which essentially characterise the smaller sales formats, cannot however be sustained in the large Mercedes-Benz Centres: Here large wall panes and surfaces covered with communications-media structure the façades and, at the same time, ensure regulated and controllable lighting conditions in the interior of the building.

With this background regarding its function, the size of these building projects basically show a serious communication problem: Those who have been halfway attentively following the architectural debates over the last few decades will recall that the complex conditions of creating large modern architectonic and urban developmental projects have not only called

Bauherren und Nutzern in Frage gestellt haben. Die Baupraxis und die Entwicklungen der Finanz- und Immobilienmärkte erzeugten gleichzeitig auch neue Vorstellungen von (Kunden-) Nutzen und Brauchbarkeit, von Prozess- und Ergebnisoptimierung.

Das Spektrum dessen, was insbesondere in der Wirtschaftsarchitektur heute als funktional oder qualitätvoll gilt, hat sich dramatisch erweitert. Andererseits sind die Positionen, die da aus je spezifischen Interessenlagen vertreten werden, selten unumstritten und bedürfen meist einer moderierenden Instanz und intelligenter Vermittlungsmethoden.

Investoren und Gebäudenutzer (die heute kaum noch identisch sind) sehen ihre Erwartungen an ein Gebäude oft nur unzulänglich erfüllt. Im Gegenzug beklagen Architekten den Verlust ihres Bauherrn – jenes persönlichen Auftraggebers und Ansprechpartners, der seinerzeit noch engagiert, zielbewusst und stilsicher den Dialog über „sein" Projekt zu führen wusste. An die Stelle dieser fast schon legendären Figur sind längst korporative Bauherren getreten, die ihre Gebäude nicht selbst nutzen und manchmal nur vorübergehend besitzen. Deren Anliegen und die ihrer Kunden werden in sehr heterogen zusammengesetzten Gremien formuliert und nicht mehr direkt, sondern über Projektentwickler und -steuerer sowie Generalunter- oder -übernehmer an die Planer kommuniziert.

Die Logik der Baufinanzierung, umfangreiche „Lastenhefte", die heute bei einem Bauprojekt abzuarbeiten sind, die Vielzahl der Beteiligten im und am Planungs- und Bauprozess, nicht zuletzt die komplexen Forderungen an die nachhaltige Nutzbarkeit eines Gebäudes haben eingeschliffene Prozesse des Planens und Bauens auf den Kopf gestellt und rasant beschleunigt. Gewohnte sequentielle Abläufe erwiesen sich als zeitraubend und kostspielig. An ihre Stelle treten heute – gestützt durch moderne Informationstechnologie – synchron gesteuerte, rückgekoppelte Prozesse und Simultantechniken, die Entwurf, Planung und Bauökonomie eng verzahnen und optimieren sollen. Gleichzeitig wächst allerdings auch die Zahl der Entscheider im Baugeschehen, die als architektonische Laien den legitimen Anspruch erheben, bei der Projektplanung einbezogen zu werden. Das erzeugt neue

into question the handed-down role of architects, planners, clients and users. Building practice and the developments of the financial and estate markets, at the same time, have produced new ideas for (customer) use and usability, as well as the optimising of processes and results.

The spectrum of what is currently considered functional or qualitative in commercial architecture has grown dramatically. On the other hand the positions that represent different interests are seldom undisputed. As a rule, they need a moderating hand and intelligent bargaining for the best solution.

Investors and those using the building (these are scarcely one and the same nowadays) often see their expectations of a building inadequately fulfilled. Architects primarily complain of the loss of their clients – those personal contractors and contacts, who at the time knew how to conduct the dialogue on "their" project in a committed, decisive and style-conscious way. These almost legendary figures have long been replaced by corporate clients who will not use the building themselves and who might only own it temporarily. Their wishes and the wishes of their customers are formulated in very heterogeneously formed committees and then not communicated to the planners directly but via project developers and managers as well as general contractors.

The logics of construction financing, detailed log books which have to be worked on, the numerous amount of people involved in the planning and building process and, last but not least, the complex requirements for the sustainability of a building, have not only turned established planning and building processes upside down but also sped them up enormously. The usual sequence of events has proved time-consuming and costly. Today, with the aid of modern information technology, these have been replaced by synchronically managed feedback processes and simultaneous technologies which should closely interlink and optimise the design, planning and building economics. However, at the same time the number of decision-makers in the building process is also increasing – architectural laypeople who feel a legitimate claim to be involved

**Das geplante Brand Center
Stuttgart im Modell:
Perspektive vom Werks-
gelände Untertürkheim**

The planned Stuttgart Brand
Centre as a model:
perspective of the factory grounds
in Untertürkheim

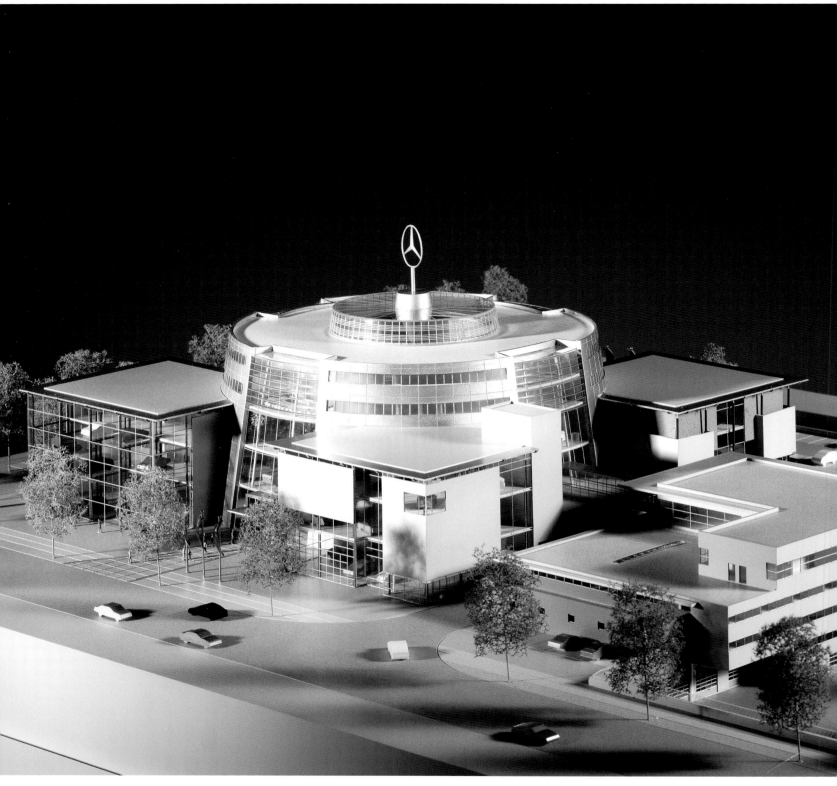

Modell des geplanten Mercedes-Benz Centers in Köln

Model of the planned Mercedes-Benz Centre in Cologne

Anforderungen und Defizite in der Planungskommunikation – und verlangt gut funktionierende Partizipationsmodelle mit visuellem Umsetzungspotential und entsprechender Aussagekraft.

Die simultane Planung mehrerer Mercedes-Benz Center für Europa war ein hinreichender und guter Anlass, innovative Werkzeuge zur Entwicklung dieser großformatigen Markenplattformen in einem technisch gestützten Dialog- und Beteiligungsverfahren zu entwickeln. Die Infrastruktur dafür bot das Mercedes Technology Center (MTC) in Sindelfingen. Hier wird mit hochgezüchteter Simulations-Software vorwiegend Fahrzeugentwicklung betrieben. Die Virtual-Reality-Technik (VR) eignet sich aber auch hervorragend dazu, räumlich-architektonische Entwürfe und Planungskonzepte visuell darzustellen, zu kommunizieren und im Dialog zwischen Architekten, Markenmanagern und -strategen, mit Vertriebsexperten, Testkunden oder Repräsentanten von Behörden zu variieren bzw. zu modifizieren.

Im Virtual Reality Center von Sindelfingen können sich die an den Großprojekten beteiligten Dialogpartner „immersiv" in die Entwürfe von Markenwelten hineinversetzen, diese durchstreifen und die Architektur auf der Grundlage der in CAD-Formaten gespeicherten Entwurfsdaten verändern. Die Simulation des Raumerlebnisses erfolgt mittels VR-Software und Videoprojektoren. Jene werfen Stereobilder auf vier, fünf oder sechs würfelförmig angeordnete Projektionsflächen, innerhalb derer sich die Betrachter aufhalten und die Bildabläufe steuern.

Die Bilder addieren sich in diesen „Cube" oder „Cave" genannten Projektionsräumen zu einem dreidimensionalen, sehr realitätsnahen Raumerlebnis – der Betrachter wird Teil des virtuellen Ambientes, in dem er sich „bewegen" und das er gegebenenfalls interaktiv verändern kann. Die Mitglieder einer Projektgruppe sind so in der Lage, Alternativen zu entwickeln, Elemente zu verschieben, zu vergrößern und zu verkleinern, Mobiliar und Exponate zu entfernen und hinzuzufügen. Sie können Farben verändern, Lichtquellen variieren, Sichtverhältnisse überprüfen, Präsentationskonzepte optimieren, die Anmutung unterschiedlicher Oberflächen testen etc.

in the planning of the project. This creates new requirements and deficits in the planning communication process and requires well-functioning participation models with a visual realisation potential and the strength of expression to go with it.

The simultaneous planning of several Mercedes-Benz Centres in Europe was a sufficient and good enough opportunity to develop innovative tools designed for the development of large-scale brand platforms in a technically supported dialogue and involvement process. The infrastructure for this was supplied by the Mercedes Technology Centre (MTC) in Sindelfingen. Here over-bred simulations software is mainly used for the development of vehicles. The virtual reality technology (VR) is however also extremely well-suited to visually depict and communicate spatial-architectural designs and planning concepts. It is also an optimal tool to vary and modify these concepts in dialogue with architects, brand managers and strategists as well as sales experts, test customers or the representatives of various authorities.

In the Sindelfingen Virtual Reality Centre, those dialogue partners involved in the large-scale projects are able to "immerse" themselves in the designs of the brand world, they can wander around them and change the architecture on the basis of the design data saved in the CAD formats. The simulation of spatial experiences is created by VR software and video projectors. These project stereo pictures onto four, five or six projection surfaces arranged in cube shapes within which observers can stay and monitor the picture sequences.

In these projection rooms, called "cubes" or "caves", the pictures create a three-dimensional and very realistic spatial experience – the observer becomes part of the virtual ambience in which he or she can "move" and interactively change if need be. The members of a project group are thus in a position to develop alternatives, to shift, enlarge and scale down elements, to remove and add furnishings and exhibits; they can alter the colour, vary light sources, check visibility, optimise presentation concepts, test the look of various surfaces and so on.

**Modell des geplanten Mercedes-
Benz Centers in Mailand**

Model of the planned Mercedes-
Benz Centre in Milan

Die Marke in den Metropolen: Mercedes-Benz Center der Zukunft

Die Initiative, Markenwelten von Mercedes-Benz in Cybertechnologie zu entwerfen, darzustellen und im strukturierten Dialog zu optimieren, hat mittlerweile einen Namen: „Mercedes-Benz Markenstudio".
Das Markenstudio ist nicht nur ein Werkzeug, mit dem heterogenes Expertenwissen verknüpft und verständlich gemacht werden kann. Die Erfahrung zeigt auch, dass sich damit Planungszeiten verkürzen und entsprechend Kosten reduzieren lassen – nicht nur im Bereich der Markenarchitektur, sondern auch im Messe- und Ausstellungsbetrieb. Es wäre wünschenswert, dass diese partizipationsfreundliche Medientechnologie bald auch Einzug in öffentliche, insbesondere kommunale Planungsprozesse und Bauprojekte hält.

The initiative of designing, depicting the brand world of Mercedes-Benz in cyber technology as well as optimising it in a structured dialogue, has now acquired a name: "Mercedes-Benz Brand Studio". The Brand Studio is not only a tool whereby heterogenous expert knowledge can be interlinked and made comprehensible. Experience also shows that planning time can be reduced further, allowing a reduction of costs – not merely in the field of brand architecture but also in the running of trade fairs and exhibitions. It would be desirable for this participation-friendly media technology to enter into the public and, in particular, communal planning processes and building projects soon.

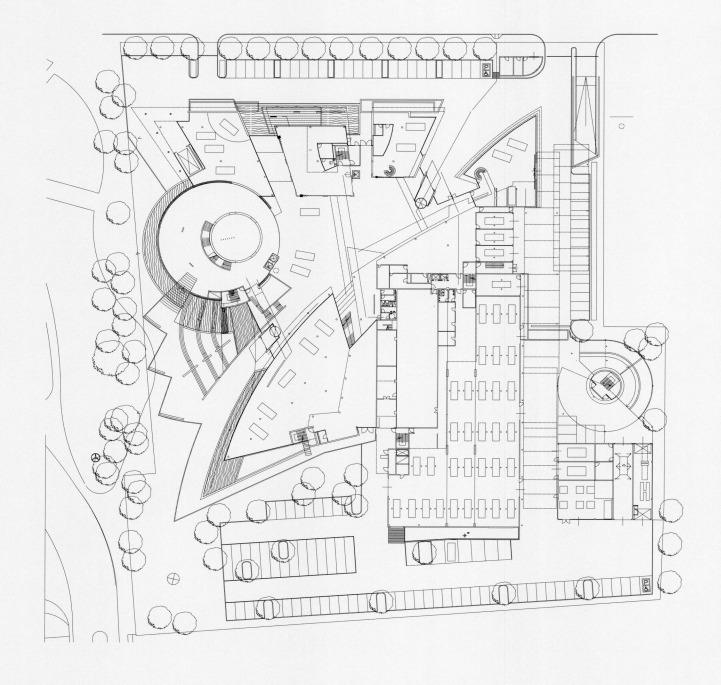

1:1000

**Grundriss und Aufsicht des
Centers in Mailand**

Plan and top view of the
Centre in Milan

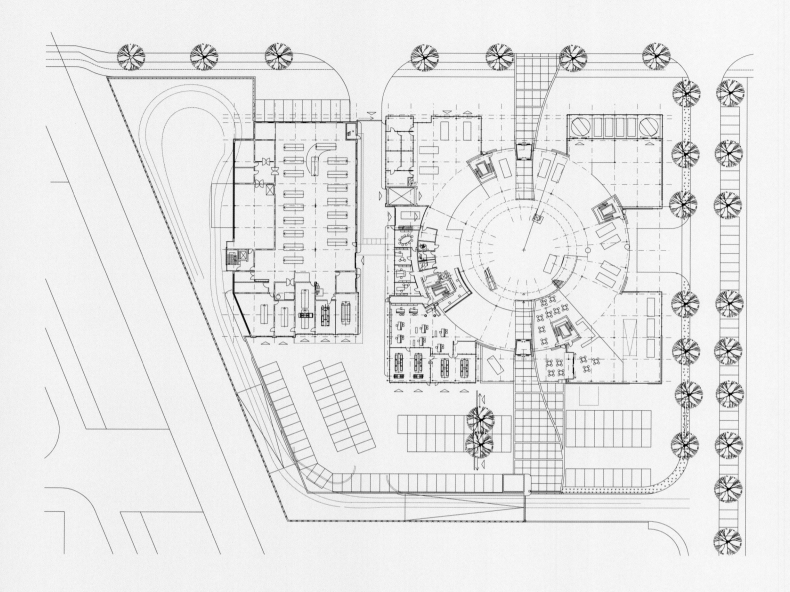

1:1000

Die Marke in den Metropolen: Mercedes-Benz Center der Zukunft

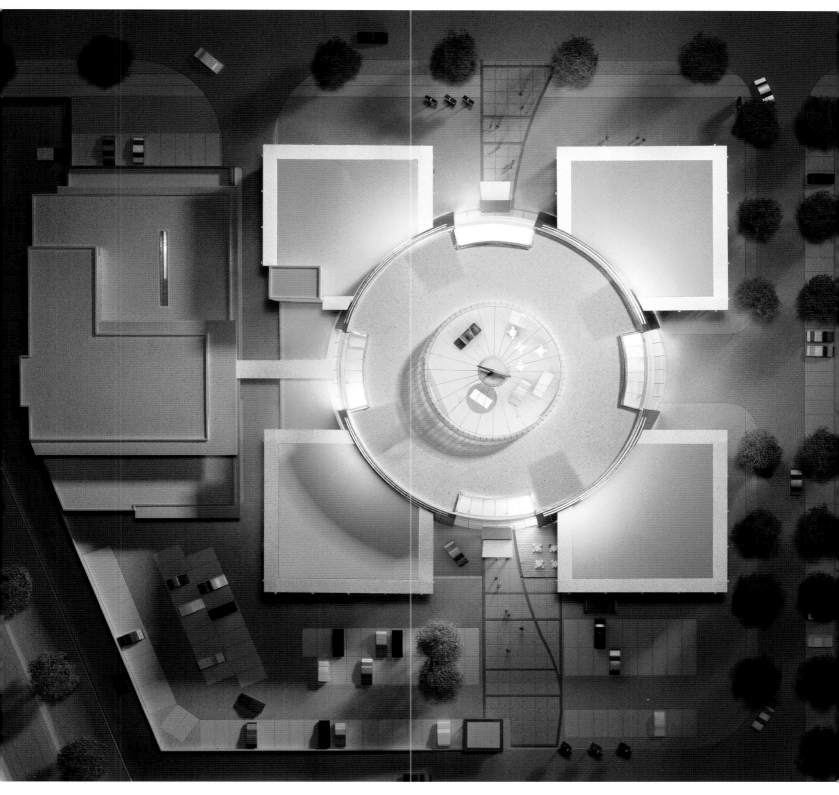

Grundriss und Aufsicht des Centers in Köln

Plan and top view of the Centre in Cologne

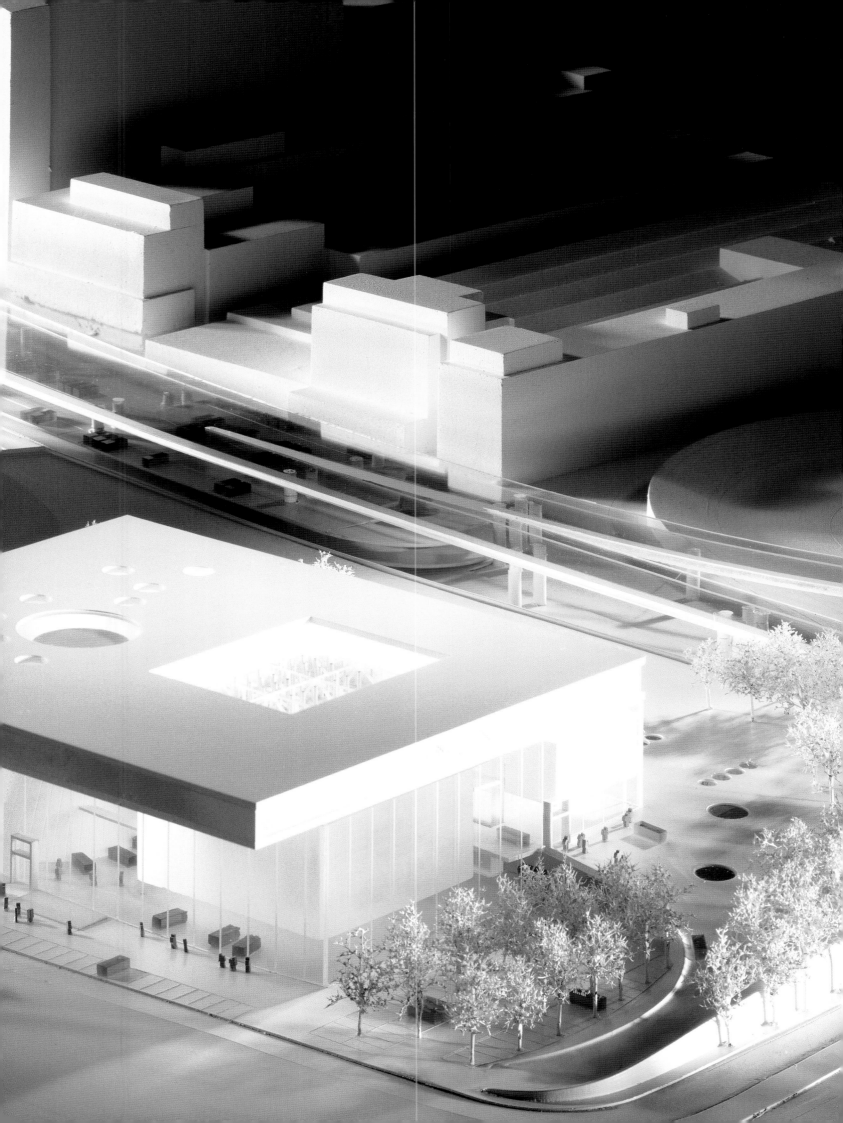

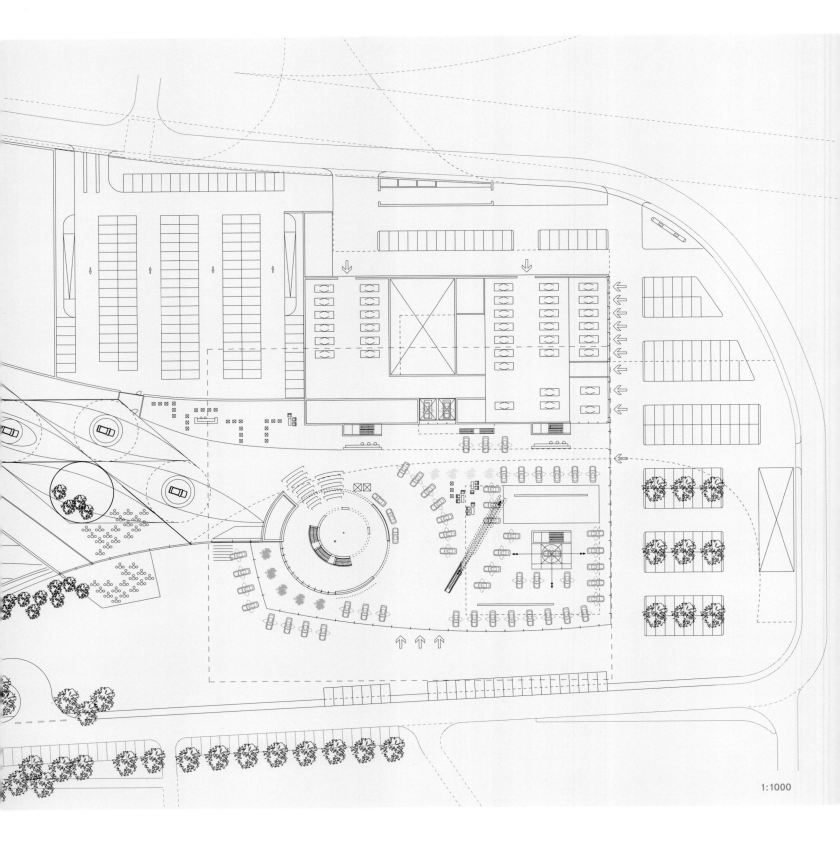

1:1000

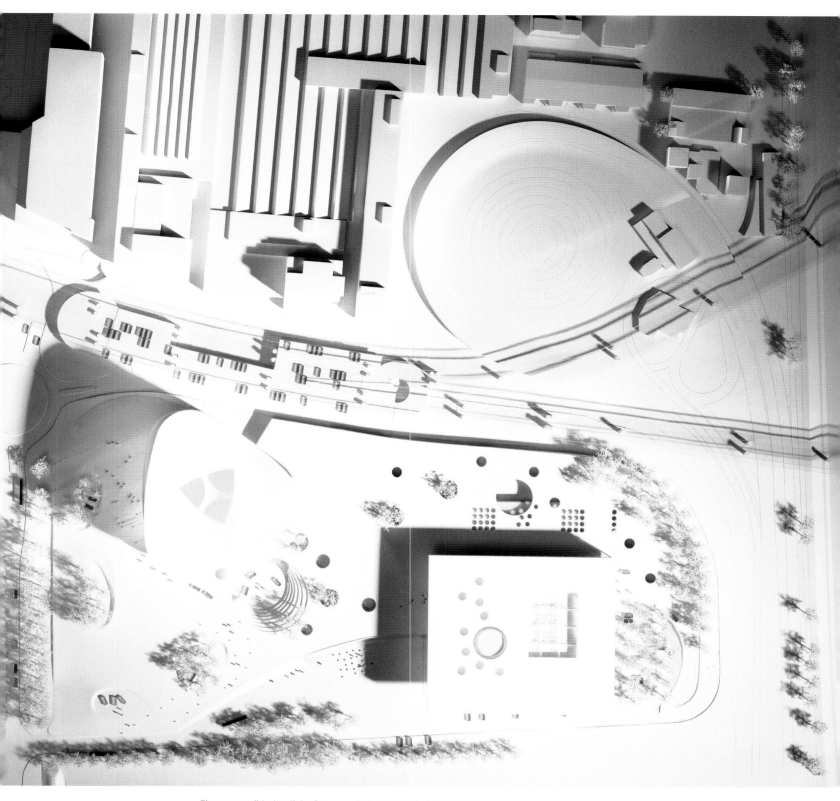

Eine enge städtebauliche Be-
ziehung mit den Werksanlagen
pflegt das neue Brand Center
am Stuttgarter Stammsitz des
Unternehmens: Die aufgestelz-
te Schnellstraße zwischen den
beiden Gebäudekomplexen
wird hier zum bekräftigenden
Symbol der Mobilität.

A close urbanistic relation to
the factory plant is maintained
by the new Brand Centre at
the Stuttgart headquarters of
the company: The stilted
motorway between the two
building complexes becomes a
reinforced symbol of mobility.

Für City-Flaneure: Mercedes-Benz Spots
For city strollers: Mercedes-Benz spots

Eine gut funktionierende
Gastronomie ist das Kernstück
des Mercedes-Benz Spots am
Berliner Kurfürstendamm.

Good gastronomy is the nucleus of the Mercedes-Benz spot
at Berlin's Kurfürstendamm.

Für City-Flaneure: Mercedes-Benz Spots

Wer am Wochenende einen Ausflug zu den Autohändlern an den Ausfallstraßen der Großstädte unternimmt, wird schnell feststellen, dass das weibliche Geschlecht im Publikum dort eher unterrepräsentiert ist. Jene aktive Sondierungsphase, die der Annäherung an eine Automarke oder dem Kauf eines Fahrzeugs meist vorausgeht, scheint Männersache zu sein, auch wenn Frauen – wie die Marktforschung belegt – bei der Wahl des Automobils in einer Paarbeziehung letztlich doch ihr Mitspracherecht geltend machen.

Mit anderen Worten: Autohäuser, in der Regel bestenfalls in City-Randlagen, meist aber an Stadträndern zuhause, haben es nicht leicht, ihr Zielgruppenpotential wirklich auszuschöpfen oder gar neue Zielgruppen anzusprechen. Spielt bei einer Marke vielleicht allein die Ungunst der Lage in Vor- und Zwischenstädten eine Rolle, mögen es bei einer anderen Marke vielleicht auch noch zusätzliche „Schwellenängste" sein, die ein breiteres Publikum davon abhalten, spontan längere Wege zu einem Autohaus zurückzulegen.

Zielgruppen nicht nur anzuziehen, sondern gewissermaßen dort abzuholen, wo sie sind – das ist die Aufgabe der Mercedes-Benz Spots, die in den letzten Jahren in zentralen Lagen großer Städte entstanden sind. Gelegen in 1A-Lagen, profitieren die Spots von den urbanen Qualitäten des Umfelds und strahlen auf diese zurück: So entstehen klein dimensionierte Markenplattformen, bei denen die unaufdringliche, fast beiläufige Markenkommunikation eine große Rolle spielt, während die Interessen des Vertriebs hier nachgeordnet sind.

Schon dieses Konzept verdeutlicht, dass Mercedes-Benz Spots, für sich genommen, keine wirtschaftlich selbsttragenden Einheiten sein können. Sie rechnen sich nur im Kontext der Marketingstrategien übergeordneter Vertriebsorganisationen, als deren „High-Street-Outlets" sie fungieren. Es geht vornehmlich um Präsenz – an zentralen städtischen Orten mit maximaler Publikumsfrequenz, mit einem dichten, hoch qualifizierten Angebot an Handel und Dienstleistungen. Ziel ist die Intensivierung des Dialogs mit dem Publikum.

For city strollers: Mercedes-Benz spots

Anyone paying a visit to car dealerships on the arterial roads in big towns at the weekend quickly comes to the conclusion that the female population is rather under-represented. All the actively exploratory phases which precede approaching a car brand or initiating the purchase of an automobile appear to be a male thing – even if, as has been proved by market research, women in a relationship do eventually exercise their right to voice their opinion in the choice of which car to buy.

In other words: As a rule, car dealerships, in the best case located on the periphery of a city but mostly on the edge of the city, do not find it easy to exhaust their target group potential or even attract new target groups. If unfavourable locations in the suburbs or between towns alone play a role with one brand, with other brands there might be additional fears of entering the showroom that prevent a broader public from spontaneously travelling a longer distance to visit one.

Thus the job of the Mercedes-Benz spots, which have been created in the central locations of large cities in the last few years, is ultimately not only to attract the target groups but, to a certain degree, also to meet them where they are. Situated in prime locations the spots tend to benefit from the urban qualities of the surroundings and reflect them back in return: small-scale brand platforms at which subtle, almost casual brand communication plays a major role whilst sales interests are of secondary importance.

This concept alone explains why the Mercedes-Benz spots, on their own are not able to support themselves financially. They are only financially viable in the context of marketing strategies of larger sales organisations for which they function as "high street outlets". The main aim is the brand presence – at central urban places maximally frequented by the public, together with a dense high-quality supply of trade and services. The ultimate goal is the intensification of dialogue with the general public.

Mercedes-Benz Spots dienen vornehmlich als urbane Treffpunkte für ein denkbar breites Spektrum an Zielgruppen. Markenkommunikation folgt hier anderen Regeln als den üblichen, weil das Publikum über sympathische Umwege – etwa gastronomische und / oder kulturelle Angebote – mit der Marke in Kontakt kommt, wenn es denn will. Denn die Atmosphäre des Mercedes-Benz Spots ist die eines Bistros oder einer Boutique: Orte, die man unbefangen betritt, wo man leger (und ohne sich bedrängt zu fühlen) verweilt, sich unterhält und unterhalten wird – und die man ebenso zwanglos wieder verlässt.

Markenstrategisch thematisiert Mercedes-Benz mit den Spots und in den Spots die Öffnung hin zu „Trendwerten" einerseits – und zu neuen, nämlich jungen Zielgruppen andererseits. Hier wird *Lifestyle* zelebriert, der das Thema Auto einbezieht, aber nicht zum beherrschenden Thema macht, der offen ist für die Erwartungen und Interessen etwa von Frauen oder Jugendlichen und der die Werte der Marke Mercedes-Benz eher assoziativ als direkt kommuniziert.

Weil Mercedes-Benz Spots Treffpunkte für Szenegänger, Shopper, Kosmopoliten, Geschäftsleute und Kulturvolk sein sollen, fungiert in der Regel die (qualitätvolle) Gastronomie als zentraler Publikumsattraktor. Um sie herum sind die herkömmlichen Funktionen des City-Showrooms und des Merchandising-Shops gruppiert, ergänzt durch Multimedia-Angebote (z.B. Internet-Terminals, Börsen-TV, Filmprojektionen etc.). All diese Elemente und Angebote sind gewissermaßen Mosaiksteine, die erst in der Addition ein Bild der Marke ergeben. Ein Bild allerdings, das nicht festgefügt ist, sondern offen für die individuellen Interpretationen und Assoziationen recht heterogener Zielgruppen.

Mercedes-Benz Spots ohne Gastronomie sind Markenboutiquen: hier dominieren naturgemäß die Funktionen des City-Showrooms und der Merchandising-Shops. Die Räumlichkeit des Spots erlaubt die Präsentation eines, allenfalls zweier Fahrzeuge. Im Bereich des Merchandising prägen hochwertige Accessoires, Reise- und Sportgepäck, Kleidung und Modellfahrzeuge das Angebot.

Mercedes-Benz spots principally serve as urban meeting points for the broadest possible spectrum of target groups. Here brand communication follows different rules from the norm as the public comes into contact with the brand through amiable circumstances – such as gastronomy and/or cultural events, if it so wishes. The atmosphere of the Mercedes-Benz spot is that of a bistro or a boutique: these are places people enter casually, where they stay awhile (without feeling pressurized), where they communicate and are entertained – and which they leave again with just as little pressure.

In terms of brand strategy Mercedes-Benz's central theme of the spots and within the spots is the opening towards "trend values" on the one hand, and the opening towards new, young target groups on the other. Here people celebrate *lifestyle* and although this includes the "car theme" it does not make it the overriding factor. It is open to the expectations and interests of women and young people; and it communicates the values of the Mercedes-Benz brand through association rather than in a direct way.

Mercedes-Benz spots are supposed to be meeting points for clubbers, shoppers, cosmopolitan and business people as well the culturally aware. Thus the high-quality gastronomy is, as a rule, the central point of attraction. The conventional functions of the city showrooms and the merchandising shops are located around this area, and they are complemented by various types of multimedia (e.g. Internet terminals, stock market TV, film projections etc.). To a certain degree, all of these elements and facilities are pieces of a mosaic, which only create an image of the brand as a whole. This image is, however, not completely fixed but open to individual interpretations and associations of quite heterogenous target groups.

Mercedes-Benz spots without gastronomy are brand boutiques: Naturally the functions of a city showroom and merchandising shop dominate here. The limited space of the spots only allows the presentation of one, at best, two vehicles. The area of merchandising consists of high-quality accessories, travel and sports luggage, clothing and model cars.

Die Marke in der City:
Mercedes-Benz Spot in Florenz

The brand in the city:
Mercedes-Benz spot in Florence

Wie Kunstobjekte: Farb- und Materialmuster im Berliner Mercedes-Benz Spot

Like objects of art: colour and material samples in the Berlin Mercedes-Benz spot

Das innenarchitektonische Konzept der Mercedes-Benz Spots setzt auf Zurückhaltung und Eleganz, auf den Einsatz hochwertiger Materialien und eine gewisse *Coolness* im Design. Die Außenwirkung, das heißt die Gestaltung der Fassade(n), nimmt selbstbewusst Bezug auf die Architektursprache des Gebäudes, respektiert aber gegebenenfalls auch historisch wertvolle Bausubstanz.

Im Konzept des Mercedes-Benz Spots kulminiert die Idee, die Marke als Gastgeber zu profilieren. Nirgendwo und zu keinem Zeitpunkt sieht sich der Besucher genötigt, etwas zu kaufen oder Verträge abzuschließen, er darf sich ganz in der Rolle des Gasts fühlen. Das ist vergleichbar mit der Rolle, die Besucher auch auf Automobilmessen spielen. Automobilmessen sind nicht zuletzt deshalb so populär, weil es dort ebenfalls in erster Linie um Markenkommunikation geht und die unmittelbaren vertrieblichen Interessen der Aussteller zurückstehen müssen. Das Publikum kennt keine Schwellenangst: ein wesentliches Argument für eine Marke, die ihren Premium-Anspruch behaupten, gleichzeitig aber neue Marktsegmente erschließen will.

The interior architectural concept of the Mercedes-Benz spots is defined by a certain reserve and elegance, with the use of high-quality materials and a degree of *coolness* in the design. The effect from the outside, that is the design of the façade(s), refers with self-confidence to the architectural language of the building, but where necessary respects the substance of historically valuable buildings.

The main idea behind the concept of the Mercedes-Benz spots is to increase the brand's profile by turning it into a host. At no time or place do visitors feel compelled to buy something or sign a contract – they are completely free to enjoy their role as a guest. This is comparable to the role that visitors play at motor shows. Motor shows are in the first instance popular because they are primarily about brand communication and the exhibitors' immediate sales interests have to take a backseat. The public is not afraid of crossing the threshold: This is an essential argument for a brand which aims to maintain its claim to premium quality and, at the same time, wishes to acquire new segments of the market.

**High Street Outlet: der
Mercedes-Benz Spot an Berlins
erster Flaniermeile**

High street outlet: the
Mercedes-Benz spot in Berlin's
top shopping street

Im Glanz edel gearbeiteter Oberflächen erstrahlt die Marke im Mercedes-Benz Spot am Berliner Kurfürstendamm: Lifestyle rund ums Auto.

The brand gleams with its sparkling and beautifully finished surfaces in the Mercedes-Benz spot in the Kurfürstendamm: lifestyle around the car.

Kühle Eleganz und Klassische Moderne – das Interieur des Florentiner „High Street Outlets"

Coolly elegant and classically modern – the interior of the Florentine "high street outlets"

Premium und Standard: Kleine und mittlere
Autohausformate in Deutschland
Premium and standard: small and middle-sized
showroom formats in Germany

**Frontansicht des Autohauses
in Lemgo**

Frontal view of the Lemgo
showroom

Premium und Standard: Kleine und mittlere Autohausformate in Deutschland

Premium und Standard: Kleine und mittlere Autohausformate in Deutschland

In kleinen und mittleren Autohäusern gelingt relativ mühelos, was in den größeren Formaten immer gleich eine strategische Herausforderung des Marketings und der Markenkommunikation ist: eine sehr direkte, alle gesellschaftlichen Schichten und Generationen umfassende Kundenansprache. Alle Dimensionen sind in den Autohäusern kleinerer Städte und auf dem „flachen Land" überschaubarer. Manches ist deshalb leichter zu handhaben – aber in der Erfolgsperspektive auch stärker abhängig vom individuellen Stil der wirtschaftlich selbstständigen Vertriebspartner.

Diesseits der Großstädte ist das Verhältnis der Händler- und Servicebetriebe zu ihren Zielgruppen und Kunden grundsätzlich direkter und persönlicher: die soziale Struktur ist kleinräumiger geordnet, die Verknüpfung und der Integrationsgrad gesellschaftlicher Gruppierungen dichter bzw. höher. Kurz gesagt: Man kennt sich, man trifft sich häufiger an den unterschiedlichsten Orten und zu vielfältigen Anlässen. Im Milieu kleinerer Städte oder großstadtferner Regionen spielen persönliche Netzwerke auch und gerade im Wirtschaftsleben eine wichtige Rolle.

Auf unser Thema bezogen heißt das: Der Systemgedanke in der Kommunikation der Marke Mercedes-Benz und im architektonischen Corporate Design ihrer Vertriebssysteme funktioniert in regionalen Strukturen unter anderen Bedingungen als in großstädtischen Märkten. Das rührt sicher nicht an die Grundfesten eines international aufgestellten Brandings. Immerhin aber dürften in kleinräumigeren und entsprechend überschaubaren Regionen Kundenerwartungen – seien sie nun an den Metzger oder an den Autohändler gerichtet – immer etwas persönlicher eingefärbt sein als in Metropolen. Deren persönlicher Stil und Auftreten prägt auch jenseits des Betriebs auf breiter gesellschaftlicher Ebene das Image nicht nur des Unternehmens, sondern auch das der dahinter stehenden Marke.

Das Systemdesign der Autohäuser von Mercedes-Benz zeichnet sich nicht zuletzt dadurch aus, dass es im wörtlichen und übertragenen Sinn Raum lässt für die

Premium and standard: small and middle-sized showroom formats in Germany

What always becomes a great strategic challenge for marketing and brand communication in larger car showroom formats comes to pass relatively easily in small and middle-sized ones: a very direct address to the customer overreaching all societal classes and generations. On the whole, all the dimensions of showrooms in smaller cities and in the country are more manageable. However, success is much more heavily dependent on the individual style of the independent sales partners.

Outside the big cities, the relationship between dealers and service centres and their target groups and customers is basically more direct and personal. The social structure is on a smaller scale and the level of integration of different social groups is significantly higher. People know each other and they meet more often in different places and on varied occasions. Here, in the smaller towns and regions located further away from larger cities, personal networks play an important role in the economic life.

Pertaining to our theme, this means that Mercedes-Benz's systematic brand communication and the architectural corporate design of its sales systems function under different conditions in regional structures than in big urban markets. This is most definitely not going to shake the foundations of the internationally oriented branding. However, in the smaller regions customer expectations, whether in relation to the butcher or the car dealer, will always tend to be more personal than in a big metropolis. Their personal style and presentation reflect the company and brand image on a much wider social scale.

One of the remarkable features of the system design of the Mercedes-Benz showrooms is that it allows – both literally and figuratively speaking – room for the personal "signatures" of the sales partners in the daily running of their business: not too much and not too little. The mandatory elements of the *brand architecture* (and the consultancy service

persönlichen „Handschriften" der Vertriebspartner im geschäftlichen Betriebsalltag: nicht zu viel und nicht zu wenig. Die verbindlichen Elemente der *Brand Architecture* (und der damit verbundene Beratungs-Service) sind so prägend, dass es zu folkloristischen Entgleisungen nicht kommen kann – mögen das nun Gestaltungsvorgaben lokaler oder regionaler Bauämter sein oder auch spezielle Ausstattungswünsche der Vertriebspartner. Andererseits lässt das modulare System auch genügend Raum, um in der Architektur etwa regionalistische Akzente zu setzen: Ein Betrieb im Schwarzwald hat, wenn die regionale Bautradition das nahe legt, durchaus die Möglichkeit, bei der Gestaltung der Gebäudefassaden Holz einzusetzen – etwa in Gestalt horizontaler Sonnenschutzblenden oder bei der Verkleidung der Werkstattgebäude.

An kleinstädtischen Standorten oder in ländlichen Regionen sind die Händler- und Werkstattbetriebe von Mercedes-Benz in besonderem Maß stadtbildprägend – sowohl an zentral gelegenen Standorten wie auch in ausgelagerten Gewerbegebieten. Hier sind der Anspruch und die Chance, mit guter Architektur Flagge zu zeigen – für das Unternehmen und die Marke! – besonders groß, da der ästhetische Standard der gebauten Umgebung meist unterdurchschnittlich ist und die relative Kleinräumigkeit des städtischen Umfelds bzw. die naturräumliche Umgebung andererseits aber nach einer gut proportionierten, sauberen und klaren Architektur verlangt.

Das modular aufgebaute System der Mercedes-Benz Architektur bietet vielfältige Möglichkeiten, sich alternativ für kompakte oder auch stark differenzierte Gebäudeformen und -geometrien zu entscheiden. Viele kleine und mittelgroße Autohäuser haben sich für den Bau klassisch dimensionierter und gegliederter Pavillons entschieden, mit rechteckigen Grundrissen, deren Straßenfronten ein klares, unkompliziertes Bild liefern.

Wo die Umgebung es verlangt oder nahelegt, findet man mehr oder minder aufgelöste Ensembles aus getrennten oder auch ineinander geschobenen Baukörpern, mit gestaffelten oder geschwungenen Fassaden. Seltener sind runde Baukörper mit starkem Signalcharakter. Sie machen vor allem dort Sinn,

associated with it) are relatively strict. Folkloristic *faux pas*, like designs from local or regional building authorities or specific decoration requests from sales partners, are practically impossible. On the other hand, however, the modular system leaves enough room for regional accents to be displayed in the architecture. In the case of a regional building tradition, such as in the Black Forest, the company has the possibility to include wood in the façade, for example in the design of horizontal sun blinds or in the cladding of a workshop.

In smaller cities and more rural regions, Mercedes-Benz dealer rooms and workshops leave a significant mark on the cityscape – in central locations, as well as in outlying industrial zones. They offer an excellent standard and opportunity of raising the profile of both the company and the brand through good architecture. The aesthetical standard of the surrounding buildings can often be below average, but the small scale and natural setting requires, on the other hand, a well-proportioned, clear and clean architecture.

The modular system of the Mercedes-Benz architecture offers many varied alternative possibilities for either compact or intricate building geometries. Many small and medium-sized showrooms have opted for pavilions with classic dimensions and structure. They have rectangular ground plans and clear, simple street façades.

Depending on the individual requirements of the local setting, the buildings can be more or less compact, the modules more or less nested, and the fronts curved or graduated. Round buildings with a strong iconic character are more rare. They are especially effective when the urban context or the landscape require a particularly strong accent.

Whichever building form is chosen, the standardised architectural elements ensure that all these buildings have an homogenous, recognisable image. The interior design is more rigorous and consistent. The use of colours and materials, as well as the choice of furniture and displays are

Die Gestaltung der Fassaden der Niederlassung Freudenstadt ist ein Reflex auf lokale Bautraditionen: Die Sonnenschutzlamellen sind aus Schwarzwaldholz.

The design of the façade at the subsidiary in Freudenstadt is a reflex of the local building tradition: The lamellar sunshades are made of Black-Forest timber.

Modellpräsentation im mittleren Format: Autohaus in Freudenstadt

Model presentation in a middle-sized format: showroom in Freudenstadt

wo der Stadt- oder Landschaftsraum nach einem markanten Akzent verlangt.

Welche Bauform auch immer gewählt wird – die standardisierten Architekturelemente geben all diesen Bauten ein einheitliches, wiedererkennbares Erscheinungsbild. Stringenter und durchgängiger ist die Gestaltung der Innenräume – sowohl was den Einsatz von Farben und Materialien angeht wie auch die Verwendung von einheitlichem Mobiliar und standardisierten Displays. Stilistische Differenzen ergeben sich meist zufällig: im Arrangement der Ausstellungsstücke in den Vitrinen (Merchandising), in der zahlenmäßigen Bestückung des Raums mit Display-Elementen oder im Einsatz von Pflanzen. Die im Verhältnis zu den großen Mercedes-Benz Centern bescheidenen räumlichen Verhältnisse zwingen zu größerer Disziplin bei der Ausstattung der Ausstellungsräume. Sie sollen großzügig wirken und nicht durch zu viel Mobiliar vollgestellt sein.

Bemerkenswert ist bei all den kleineren Autohausformaten die Tatsache, dass deren Erscheinungsbild keinerlei „Schwellenängste" erzeugt, sie vielmehr einladend und gastlich wirken. Dies ist für eine Premium-Marke wie Mercedes-Benz besonders wichtig – erst recht, seit in verstärktem Maß auch jüngere Zielgruppen erreicht werden sollen.

standardised. Stylistic differences are usually coincidental; for example, how the exhibits are arranged in the display cases (merchandising) or how many display elements are being used or what type of plants are chosen. In contrast with the big Mercedes-Benz Centres, these comparatively modest spaces require significantly more decorating discipline. Above all, they should have a spacious appearance and not be cluttered with too much furniture.

What is particularly noticeable is the fact that none of the smaller showrooms ever appear unwelcoming; moreover, they create a much more hospitable impression. For a premium brand like Mercedes-Benz this is particularly important, especially since its aim is to increasingly target younger audiences.

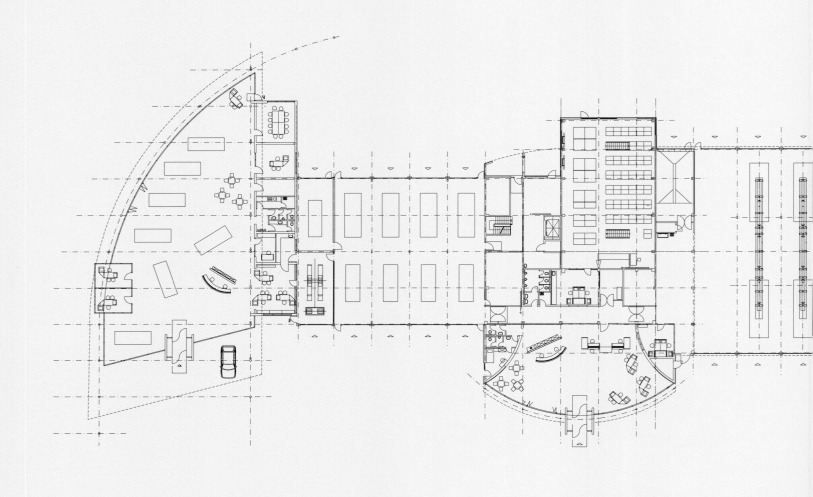

**Einer linearen Raumorgani-
sation folgt die Architektur des
Autohauses in Lemgo.**

The architecture of the
Mercedes-Benz showroom in
Lemgo displays a linear spatial
organisation.

Premium und Standard: Kleine und mittlere Autohausformate in Deutschland

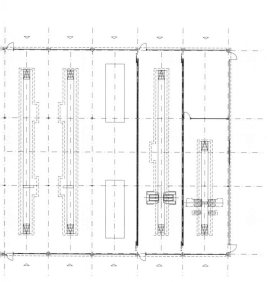

1:500

Premium und Standard: Kleine und mittlere Autohausformate in Deutschland

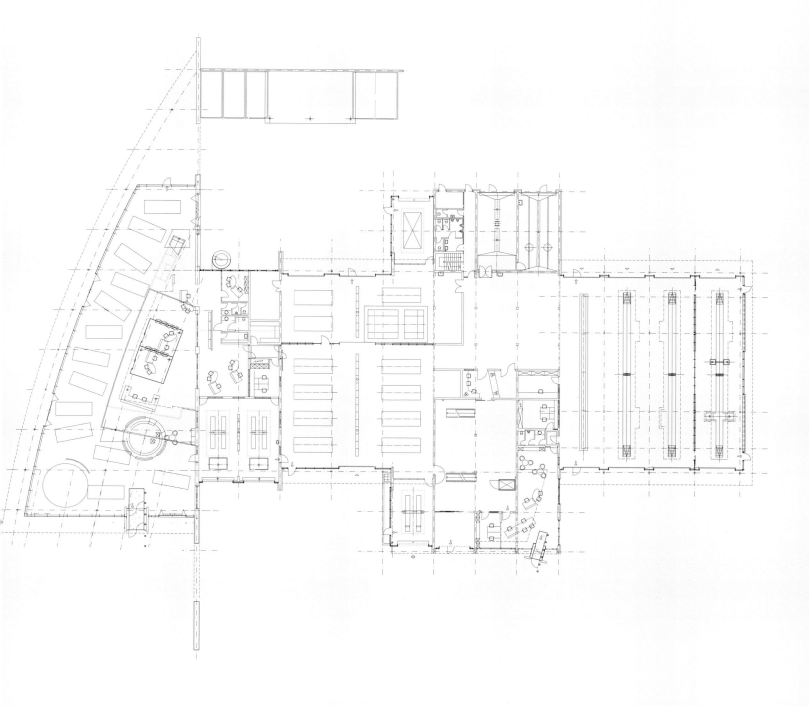

1:500

Ansichten und Grundriss des Autohauses in Freudenstadt. Sie belegen die formale Variationsbreite und Anpassungsfähigkeit der Gestaltungsmodule; die identitätsbildende Charakteristik des Systems bleibt unangetastet.

Views and plan of the showroom in Freudenstadt. They verify the formal breadth of variation and flexibility of the design modules; the identitycreating characteristic of the system remains untouched.

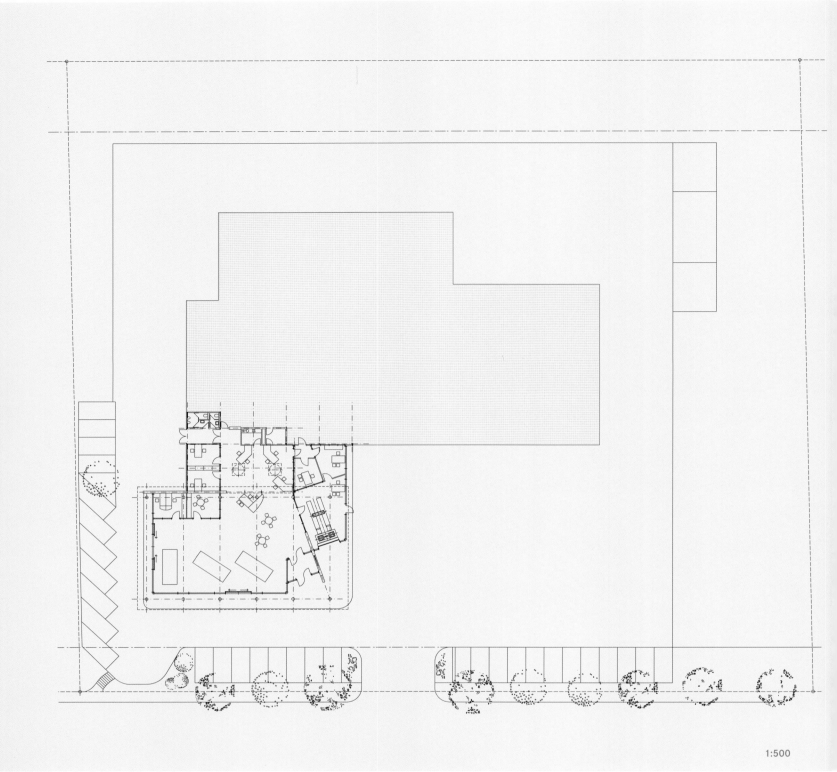

1:500

Ein in klassischem Stil
proportionierter Schauraum
verleiht dem baulichen
Bestand des Autohauses
Alsfeld ein neues, sympathi-
sches „Gesicht".

A showroom with classical
proportions lends the structure
of the Alsfeld Centre a pleasant
new "face".

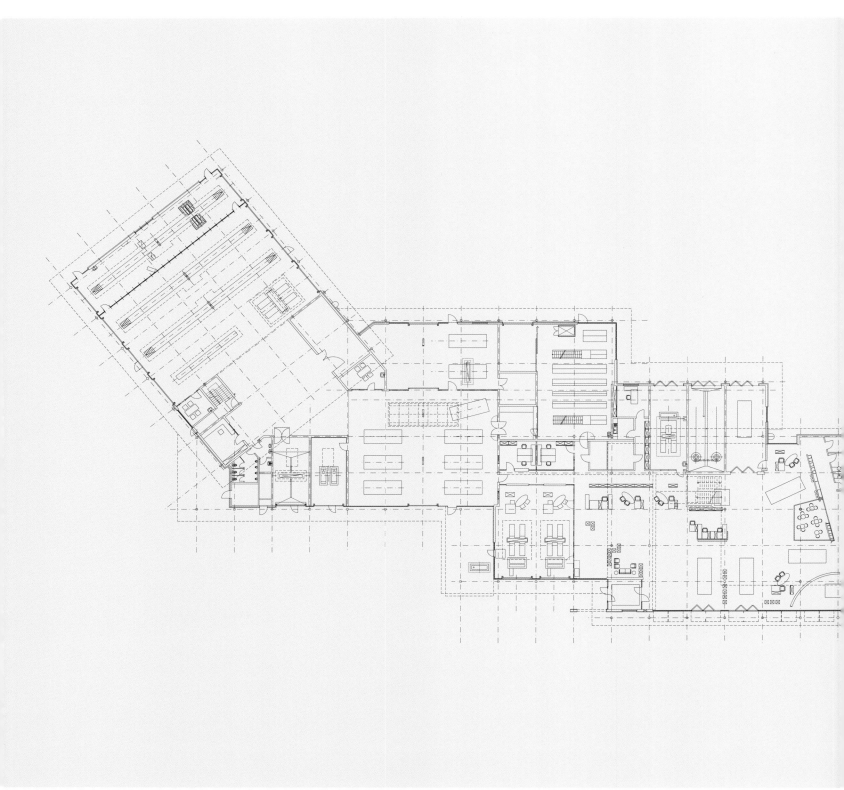

Die Topografie und der
Zuschnitt des Grundstücks
bestimmten im badischen
Bretten die Konfiguration der
Baukörper. Aus der Staffelung
der Fassaden wurde ein auffälliges Portalmotiv entwickelt.

The topography and cut of
the grounds determine the
configuration of the building
in Bretten, Baden. An eye-
catching portal motif was
developed from the graduation
of the façades.

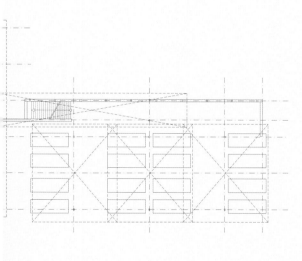

1:500

Premium und Standard: Kleine und mittlere Autohausformate in Deutschland

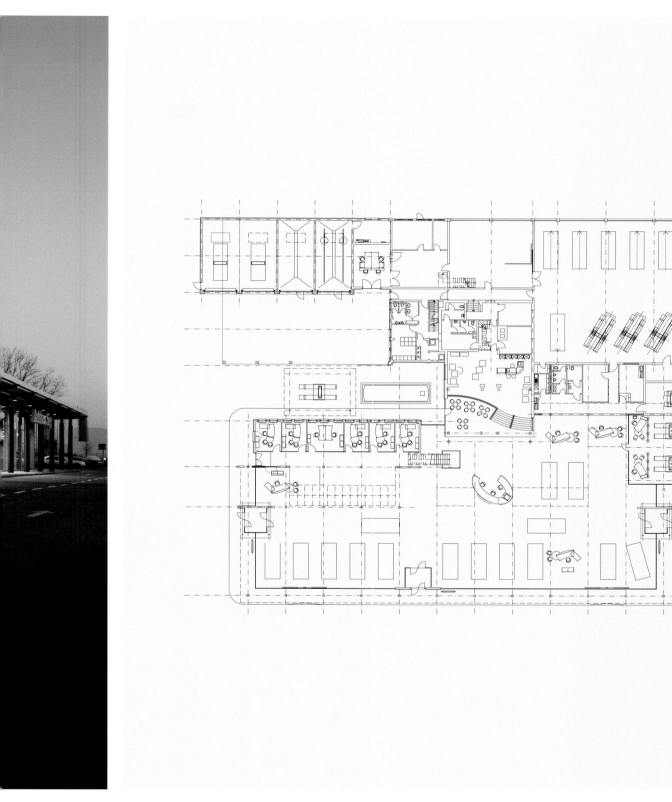

1:500

**Schauraum mit drei gleich-
wertig gestalteten Eingängen:
Autohaus in Minden**

The showroom in Minden with
three entrances, each designed
with equal importance.

Premium und Standard: Kleine und mittlere Autohausformate in Deutschland

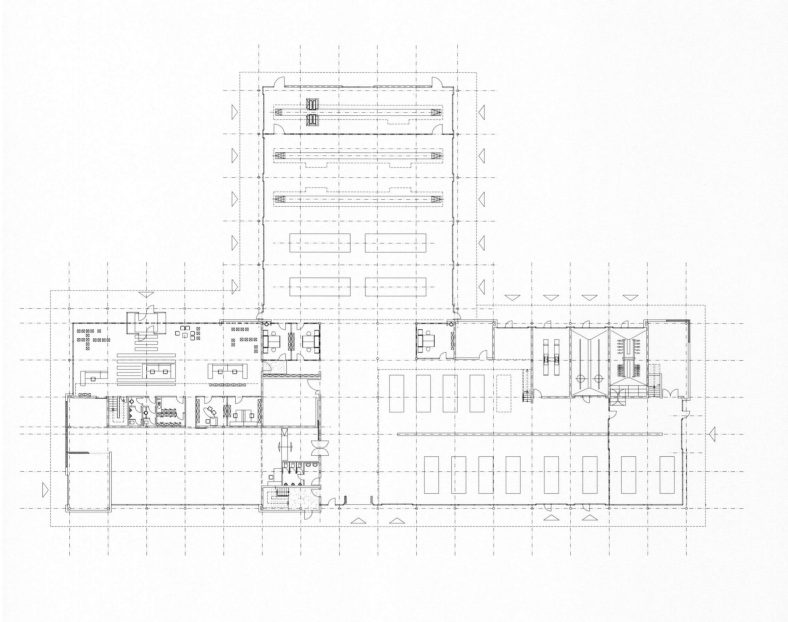

1:500

**Crailsheim: Grundriss und
Details des Interieurs (links)**

Crailsheim: plan and details
of the interior (left)

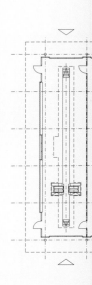

Premium und Standard: Kleine und mittlere Autohausformate in Deutschland

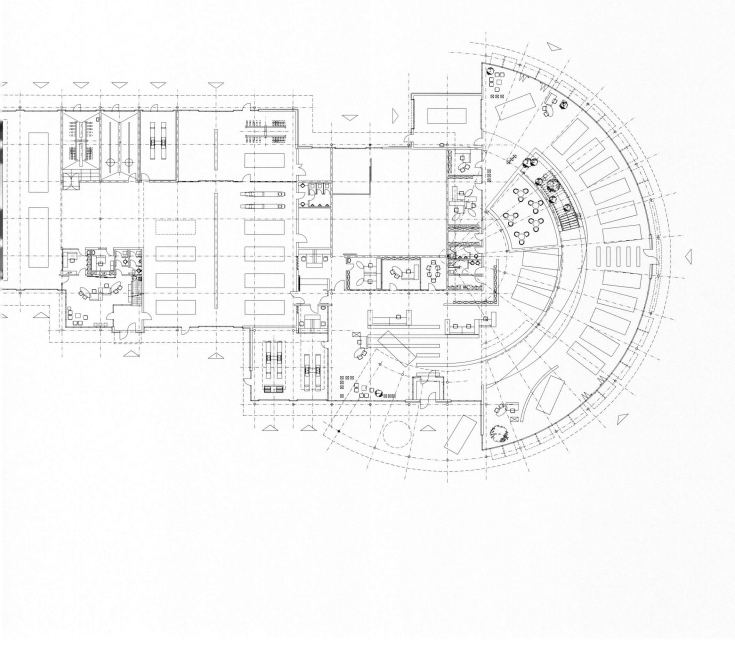

1:500

Der geometrisch ausdifferen-
zierte Baukörper des Autohauses in Schwäbisch Hall
bietet ein abwechslungs-
reiches Erscheinungsbild.

The geometrically differentiated building of the showroom
in Schwäbisch Hall offers a
varied appearance.

Mercedes-Benz in Europa
Mercedes-Benz in Europe

Unter den Gipfeln des Tessin:
Mercedes-Benz Autohaus
in Lugano

Beneath the peaks of Tessin:
Mercedes-Benz showroom
in Lugano

Mercedes-Benz in Europa

Mercedes-Benz in Europa

Neue, gemäß den CI-Grundsätzen gestaltete Mercedes-Benz Autohäuser in Europa entstanden in den letzten Jahren mehrheitlich dort, wo sich nach den politischen Umbrüchen der frühen neunziger Jahre auch dynamische neue Märkte entwickelten: in den ost- und südosteuropäischen Staaten. In diesen Regionen geht es weniger um die Pflege einer etablierten Marke als um den Aufbau und die stabile Präsenz des Markenbilds.

Unter dem Aspekt, dass dem Image der Marke Mercedes-Benz in diesen jungen Märkten ein handfester, solider „Unterbau" an Ausdruck und Tradition verschafft werden soll, gewinnt die konsequente Umsetzung der Gestaltungsleitlinien, die den neuen Autohausformaten von Mercedes-Benz zu Grunde liegen, besondere Bedeutung. Die Chance, mit qualitätvoller Architektur im Bild der Städte ein besonders hervorstechendes und aussagekräftiges Signal zu setzen, ist in osteuropäischen Regionen derzeit groß.

Das Autohaus als umgedrehter, weit auskragender, bis unters Dach verglaster Kegelstumpf: Mit diesem kompakten und doch sehr transparenten Volumen setzt die Mercedes-Benz Vertretung in Moskau an einem innerstädtischen Standort ein sehr auffälliges Zeichen. Die Fahrzeuge werden hier auf drei Ebenen präsentiert; in den Obergeschossen sind sie als umlaufende Galerien ausgebildet. Das Säulenmotiv ist im und am Gebäude – es wird von flach gehaltenen Bauten für den Service-Bereich flankiert – die gestalterische Dominante: paarweise halten die blauen Stützen das weit auskragende Dach, wobei die Rundung der Glasfront jeweils zwischen ihnen verläuft.

Das Mercedes-Benz Autohaus im polnischen Sosnowiec besteht aus drei winkelig ineinander geschobenen Rechtecksfiguren, für die der Ausstellungsbereich mit dem Kundenempfang als Klammer dient. Diese Planfigur übersetzt das Konzept des „Vertriebssterns" gewissermaßen wörtlich in Architektur.

Das Mercedes-Benz-Autohaus in Ekaterinenburg entstand unter der gleichen Regie wie das in Moskau. Der Grundriss – ein Rechteck mit einem vorgesetzten Kreissegment als Schaufassade – integriert Verkaufs-

Mercedes-Benz in Europe

New Mercedes-Benz car showrooms, designed according to the company's European CI standards, have been created primarily in Eastern and Southern European countries, where political changes in the early nineties were responsible for the development of dynamic new markets. In these regions it is less a question of cultivating an established brand than of building up the brand image and maintaining its stable presence. This fundamental work.

In these young markets, a consistent implementation of the design guidelines of the new Mercedes-Benz car showrooms is important for giving the brand a solid "foundation", combining expression and tradition. At present, Eastern European regions offer a good opportunity to create an expressive and high-quality city architecture.

The showroom is a prominent glass cone stump. With this compact but very transparent volume, the Mercedes-Benz representatives in Moscow have created a very prominent landmark located in the city centre. Here, the vehicles are displayed on three exhibition levels. On the upper floors there are surrounding galleries. The column motif dominates both the inside and outside of the building and is flanked by flat service buildings. The blue twin columns with the rounded glass front between them support the overhanging roof.

The Mercedes-Benz showroom in Ekaterinenburg was designed under the same direction as the one in Moscow. The ground plan – a rectangle with a set-forward circular segment as a display-façade – integrates sales areas, workshops and storage area in a very compact, closed figure. The combination of glass and metal lends the façades a solid, representative appearance: it was not by chance that the building was chosen as the scene for a meeting between the Russian Prime Minister Putin and the German Chancellor Schröder.

The Mercedes-Benz car showroom in Polish Sosnowiec consists of three nesting rectangles, which are connected by the exhibition area housing customer

räume, Werkstätten und Lager in einer sehr kompakten, geschlossenen Planfigur. Die Fassaden wirken durch die Kombination von Glas und Metall solide und repräsentativ: Das Gebäude wurde nicht zufällig zum Schauplatz eines Treffens zwischen dem russischen Ministerpräsidenten Putin und Bundeskanzler Schröder.

Die geschwungenen Konturen an der Frontseite der Mercedes-Benz Vertretung im kroatischen Zagreb erinnern ein wenig an die expressiven Architekturentwürfe der russischen Avantgarde des frühen 20. Jahrhunderts, aber auch an Skizzen und Bauten von Erich Mendelsohn. Das Gebäude erstreckt sich weit in die Tiefe des Grundstücks. Hier, im ausgedehnten Service-Bereich für Pkw und Nutzfahrzeuge, wechselt die Architektursprache, wird streng kubisch und „sachlich" in der Tonalität.

Die „Landschaftstauglichkeit" der Markenarchitektur von Mercedes-Benz erweist sich unter anderem an zwei neueren Autohäusern im schweizerischen Lugano und in Korinth. Die zeitgenössische Architektur des Tessin ist einerseits sehr anerkannt; andererseits ist die Industriearchitektur in den Talsohlen oft von höchst durchschnittlicher, ja dürftiger Qualität.

Das Mercedes-Benz Autohaus in Lugano-Pazzallo steht in einer Talsenke: ein gut proportionierter Pavillon, der nicht von der Straßenfront erschlossen wird, sondern von der Seite her. An der rechten Flanke des Gebäudes bilden eine Reihe paralleler Tonnendächer eine Art Pergola – überdachte Pkw-Stellplätze, die mit dem Autohaus zusammen eine „fünfte Fassade" bilden.

Berge bilden auch das Panorama eines neuen Mercedes-Benz Autohauses in Korinth. Es steht frei, die Topografie gewährt eine exponierte Lage, und so war es nahe liegend, eine runde Grundrissform für den *Showroom* zu wählen. Ein weißer, zweistöckiger Riegel verbindet das Gebäude mit dem diskret in den Hintergrund gerückten Servicebereich. Mit seinen Säulen provoziert der Rundbau die Assoziation eines Tempelchens. Im Zentrum des Rundbaus wiederholt sich das Motiv. Mit einem „Tempietto" wurde ein besonderer Ort für die Präsentation eines Automobils geschaffen.

reception. To a certain extent, this figure literally translates the Mercedes star into architecture.

The curved fronts of the Mercedes-Benz outlet in the Croatian Zagreb are slightly reminiscent of the expressive architecture of the Russian avant-garde in the early 20th century, though are equally reminiscent of Erich Mendelsohn's sketches and constructions. The building extends far back onto the property. Here, in the extended service area for cars and utility vehicles, the architectural language changes and becomes strictly cubic and neutral in its tonality.

The suitability of the Mercedes-Benz brand architecture in terms of individual landscapes is demonstrated, for example, by two new showrooms in Swiss Lugano and in Corinth. The contemporary architecture of Tessin is, on the one hand, held in high regard; on the other hand, the industrial architecture in the valley bottoms of the Tessin landscape is often of a poorer, at best average quality.

The Mercedes-Benz car showroom in Lugano-Pazzallo is located in a valley. It is a well-proportioned pavilion accessed not from the front facing the street, but from the side. At the right flank of the building a series of parallel tunnel vaults create a kind of pergola-covered parking spaces that form a "fifth façade" together with the showroom.

Mountains also form the panoramic backdrop for a new free-standing car showroom in Corinth. The exposed location of the detached building lent itself to a circular ground plan. A white, two-storey corridor connects the building with the service area which is discretely placed in the background. The round building with its columns provokes associations with a small temple, at least in this terrain – Corinth was a very important city in the antiquity. The motif is repeated in the centre of the round building. A "tempietto" is a prominent place for presenting a car.

Die schräg gestellten Stützen
im Rund des Moskauer Schau-
raums erzeugen einen Hauch
von Zirkusatmosphäre.

The bent supports around the
Moscow showroom create
a hint of a circus atmosphere.

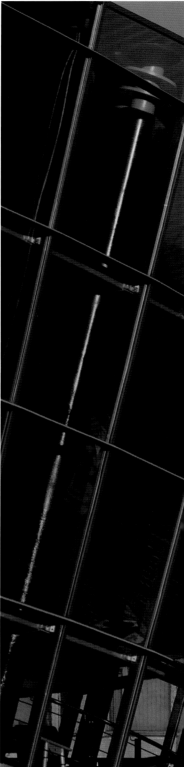

Der Mercedes-Stern als
Oberlicht: Innenansichten des
Moskauer Rundbaus

The Mercedes star as a guiding
light: inner views of the round
Moscow building

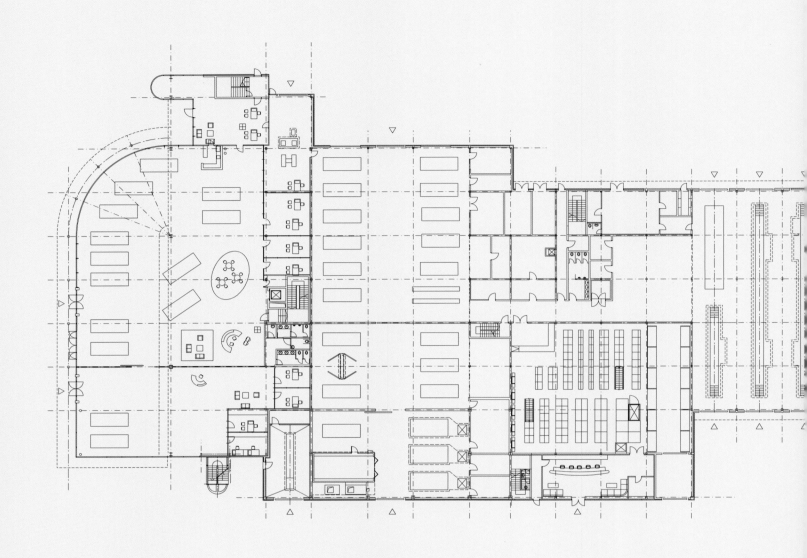

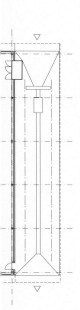

1:500

Manche Details an den Fassaden des Mercedes-Benz Autohauses in Zagreb lassen sich als Hommage an die Architektur der Klassischen Moderne interpretieren.

Many of the details on the façades of the Mercedes-Benz showroom in Zagreb can be interpreted as a homage to the architecture of the classic modern.

Mercedes-Benz in Europa

Die Lichtregie des Autohauses
in Zagreb trägt dazu bei,
die Architektur eine wenig zu
„entmaterialisieren".

The lighting of the Zagreb
showroom contributes
towards "dematerializing"
the architecture a little.

Blaue Stunde in Lugano   Blue hour in Lugano

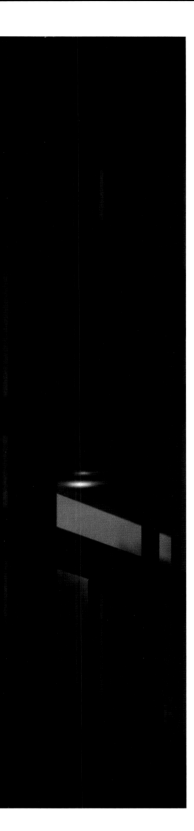

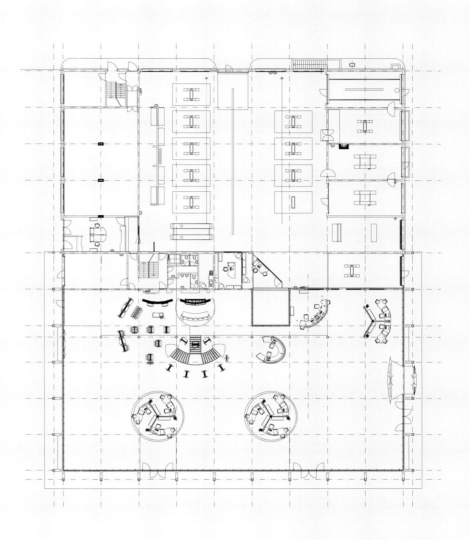

1:500

Standort Lugano: Die Tessiner
Landschaft und Baukultur stellt
besonders hohe Ansprüche
an Architektur und Städtebau.

The location of Lugano: The Tessin
landscape and building culture
require high standards of architecture and urban planning.

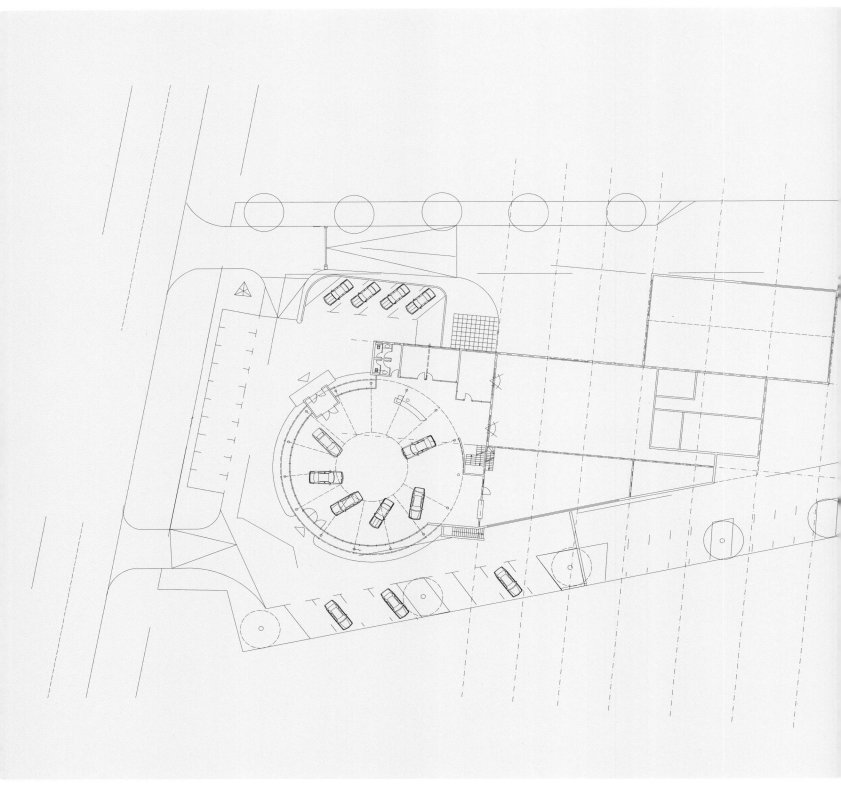

**Korinth: Kuben und Zylinder
in klassischer Landschaft**

Corinth: cubes and cylinders
in a classical landscape

1:500

Mercedes-Benz in Europa

Der Schauraum von Korinth:
Ein Rundbau mit eingestellter
Aedikula, die das Exponat
zum Mythos macht.

The showroom in Corinth:
a round building with inbuilt
Aedicula that gives the exhibit
a mythical quality.

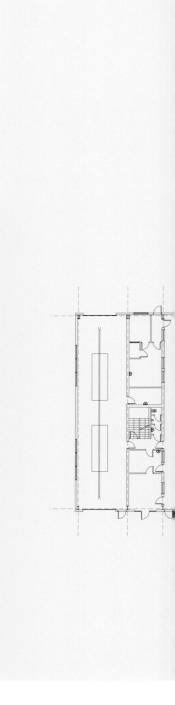

Mercedes-Benz in Europa

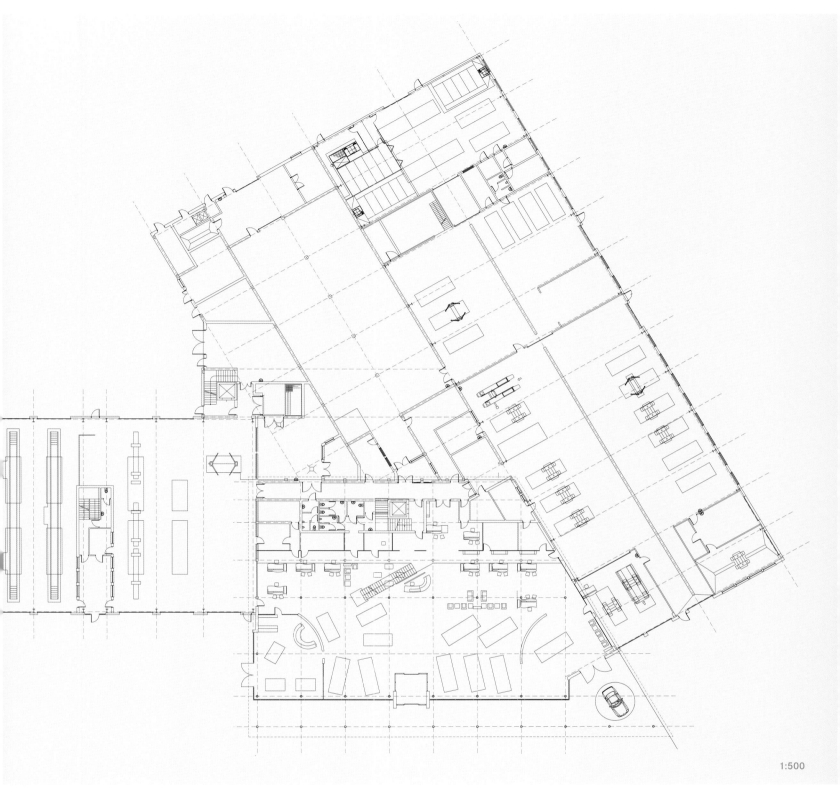

1:500

Der „Vertriebsstern", direkt
in Architektur übersetzt:
Grundriss des Autohauses
im polnischen Sosnowiec

The "sales star" directly
translated into the architecture: plan of the showroom
in Polish Sosnowiec.

Im östlichen Europa ist
Markenpflege Aufbauarbeit:
Das Mercedes-Benz Autohaus
Sosnowiec außen und innen

The care of the brand is being
built up in Eastern Europe: the
Mercedes-Benz showroom in
Sosnowiec outside and inside.

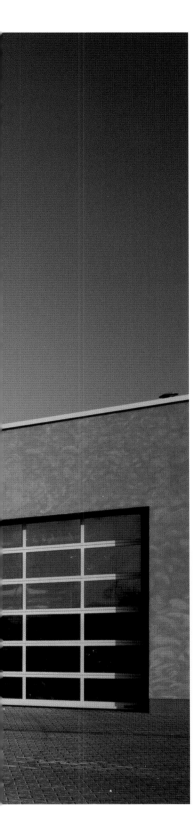

Das Autohaus Ekaterinenburg wirkt im Stadtbild so repräsentativ, dass es Brautpaaren als Kulisse für Hochzeitsbilder dient.

The showroom in Ekaterinenburg has such a representative presence in the cityscape that it is used by bridal couples as a backdrop for wedding photos.

Ein Ort mit höheren politischen Weihen: Hier traf sich
einmal der russische Minister-
präsident mit dem deutschen
Bundeskanzler.

A place with high political
significance: the Russian
Prime Minister met the
German Chancellor here.

Ferne Kontinente: Autohäuser
in Afrika, Asien und Lateinamerika
Far away continents: car dealerships
in Africa, Asia and Latin America

Das modulare Gestaltungs-
system der Mercedes-Benz
Autohausarchitektur im
Härtetest der Globalisierung:
die Vertretung im koreani-
schen Seoul.

The modular design system of
the Mercedes-Benz showroom
architecture in hard times of
globalisation: the representation
in Korean Seoul.

Ferne Kontinente: Autohäuser in Afrika, Asien und Lateinamerika

Auf dem Feld der Unternehmensberatung tummeln sich nicht wenige *Consultants*, die ihrer Klientel in Seminaren und Trainingskursen beizubringen versuchen, wie man sich als Firmenrepräsentant in anderen Kulturkreisen richtig benimmt. In der Regel geht es darum, Grundkenntnisse über fremde Sitten und Gebräuche zu erwerben – um die neu erlernten Umgangsformen bei rechter Gelegenheit „strategisch" einzusetzen.

Die Bereitschaft zur Anpassung an fremde kulturelle Standards ist meist beschränkt auf persönliche Begegnungen mit Geschäftspartnern, die in deren Heimatregionen stattfinden. Das *Branding* geht in der globalisierten Wirtschaft zumeist den umgekehrten Weg und versucht, die charakteristischen Wertedimensionen von Marken auch in fernen Kulturkreisen mit differenten Wahrnehmungsmustern möglichst ungebrochen und unverfälscht zu kommunizieren. Dazu gehört auch die Anstrengung, weltweit eine systematisch durchgestaltete „Markenarchitektur" mit hohem Wiedererkennungswert durchzusetzen.

So sinnvoll solche Markenstrategien sind – sie haben auch ihre Grenzen. Wenn etwa ein Kommunikations- oder Gestaltungsprinzip sich allzu sehr verfestigt und schließlich erstarrt, mag dies auch als Sklerotisierung der Marke selbst wahrgenommen werden. Eben dieser Gefahr einer dogmatischen Verknöcherung begegnet das Design der Mercedes-Benz Autohäuser durch seinen modularen Aufbau: indem es quasi nur Korridore der architektonischen Gestaltung vorgibt, lässt es auch formale Spielräume zur Artikulation regionaler Baukulturen.

Ein Blick auf die neu errichteten Mercedes-Benz Betriebe in Übersee, auf anderen Kontinenten, zeigt, dass der Ausdrucks- und Behauptungswille architektonischer Regionalstile nicht überall in gleichem Maß ausgeprägt ist. Mancherorts, etwa in Lateinamerika, ist davon überhaupt nichts zu spüren. Das Mercedes-Benz Autohaus in der Hauptstadt des mittelamerikanischen Kleinstaats El Salvador folgt durchgängig den eingangs beschriebenen Gestaltungsvorgaben – im Übrigen in einem

Far away continents: car dealerships in Africa, Asia and Latin America

The area of business consulting is full of *consultants*, who, in seminars and training courses, try and teach their clientele how to behave correctly as a company representative in other cultures. As a rule it is all about gaining a basic knowledge of foreign customs and habits – so these acquired manners can be used "strategically" at the right opportunity.

The willingness to adapt to foreign cultural standards is mostly restricted to personal meetings with business partners that take place in their home countries. In a global economy *branding* mainly goes completely the other way. It tries to communicate the characteristic values of the brands as purely and consistently as possible even in far-away cultures with their different patterns of perception. This includes the effort of imposing the systematic design of "brand architecture" with a high degree of recognition on a worldwide scale.

Although these brand strategies are sensible – they also have their limitations. If, for example, a communication or design principle becomes too fixed and then inflexible, it might be perceived as a sclerosis of the brand itself. It is exactly this danger of dogmatic ossification that the design of Mercedes-Benz car dealerships combats by using a modular design: as it practically only stipulates corridors of architectural design, it leaves a formal scope for the articulation of regional building styles.

A look at the newly built Mercedes-Benz offices overseas shows that the expression and assertion of architectural regional styles is not the same everywhere. In some places such as Latin America regional styles are not apparent at all. The Mercedes-Benz car dealership in the capital of the Central American state of El Salvador consistently follows the design stipulations described at the beginning – incidentally in a modern urban environment which itself shows no characteristic local colouring.

The Mercedes-Benz car dealership in North African Tunis provides a completely different picture. Towards

modernen städtebaulichen Umfeld, das seinerseits kein ausgeprägtes Lokalkolorit aufweist.

Ein ganz anderes Bild bietet das Mercedes-Benz Autohaus im nordafrikanischen Tunis. Zur Straße hin wölbt sich das verglaste Kreissegment des Ausstellungsraums mit den vertrauten blauen Säulen, die das weit vorgezogene Dach mit seinen Sonnenschutzlamellen tragen. Die abgewinkelten rückwärtigen Fronten muten dagegen mit ihren hellgelb verputzten Mauern, den blau abgesetzten und von schmalen Fenstern durchbrochenen Risaliten und einem gedrungenen runden, sich konisch nach oben verjüngenden Zentralbau wie eine modernistische Interpretation der nordafrikanischen Berber-Architektur an: sehr diskret, sehr diszipliniert, ohne folkloristischen Duktus.

Einen recht freizügigen Umgang mit den Gestaltungsrichtlinien und -modulen zeigt die innerstädtische Zentrale der Mercedes-Benz Vertretung im südkoreanischen Seoul. Dieses Haus, gelegen an einer großen Straßenkreuzung, repräsentiert Freestyle-Architektur – mit Details, die ein wenig an den frühen Frank Gehry und seine kalifornischen Strandhäuser erinnern.

Das Autohaus ist aus verschiedenen geometrischen Elementarfiguren zusammengesetzt. Eine nahezu quadratische, mit Milchglaspaneelen verkleidete Büroetage „schwebt" über zwei konventionell verglasten Ausstellungsebenen. Optischen Halt erfährt sie durch zwei schmale, weit über den Komplex hinausragende Turmbauten und die bekannten blauen Metallsäulen vor der Glasfassade, die hier allerdings wesentlich kräftiger als gewohnt ausfallen müssen.

Aus der Büroetage schiebt sich eine blaue, trapezförmige Kanzel heraus, über der ein Flugdach schwebt: Platz für ein Ausstellungsfahrzeug in luftiger Höhe. Als formales Gegengewicht zur Kanzel fungiert an dieser Front ein zweistöckiges, gläsernes Halbrund, das die dort ausgestellten Fahrzeuge für Passanten und Autofahrer an der Kreuzung besser zur Geltung bringt.

In dieser metropolitanen Architektur ist keine regionale Mentalität identifizierbar: Das Prinzip Collage ist längst universell in Gebrauch, so auch in Seoul.

the street the circular segment of the exhibition area is curved and made of glass with the familiar blue pillars which support the protruding roof with its sun-protection slats. The angled back, however, has light-yellow plaster walls and blue ornamental sections projecting from the main body of the building, interspersed with narrow windows. It includes a sturdy, conically-shaped central building which narrows towards the top. This looks like a modern interpretation of North African Berber architecture: very discreet, very disciplined and devoid of folkloristic diction.

The Mercedes-Benz inner-city head office in South Korea's Seoul is an example of a fairly free interpretation of the design guidelines and modules. This building is situated at a large crossroads and represents freestyle architecture. Its details are somewhat reminiscent of the early Frank Gehry and his Californian beach houses.

The building consists of various geometric elements. An almost square office floor, clad with frosted-glass panels, "floats" above two conventionally glassed exhibition levels. The floor is visually supported by two narrow towers, which extend far beyond the whole complex, and the blue metal columns in front of the glass façade, which for this construction have to be considerably stronger than usual.

The office floor is extended by a blue, trapezium-shaped platform with a suspended roof, which provides room for an exhibition vehicle at a dizzy height. At this front a two-storey half circle made of glass provides a formal contrast and shows the exhibited vehicles to their best advantage for passers-by and drivers at the crossroads.

In this metropolitan architecture no regional mentality can be identified: the "collage" principle has been utilised across the universe, including Seoul.

Im Mercedes-Benz Autohaus von San Salvador (oben) werden Personenwagen und Nutzfahrzeuge unmittelbar nebeneinander präsentiert; unten die Straßenfront des Autohauses in Tunis

In the Mercedes-Benz showroom in San Salvador (above) passenger cars and commercial vehicles are presented right next to each other; below the street front of the showroom in Tunis.

Der Mercedesstern als
Architekturmotiv: in Tunis als
Grundrissfigur angedeutet

The Mercedes star as an
architectural motif in Tunis –
hinted at as a plan figure.

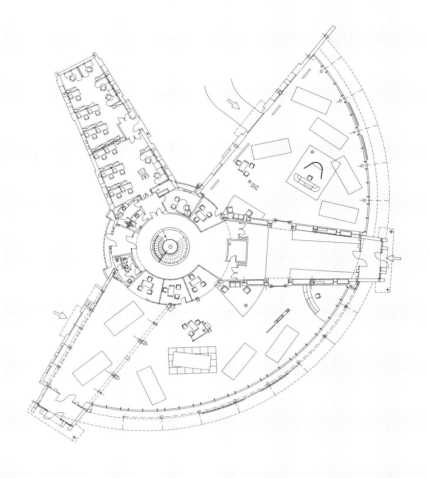

1:500

Ferne Kontinente: Autohäuser in Afrika, Asien und Lateinamerika

Tunis: Jenseits der standardisierten Schaufassade setzen
sich regionalistische Stil-
elemente durch.

Tunis: On the other side of the
standardised façades regional
stylistic elements appear.

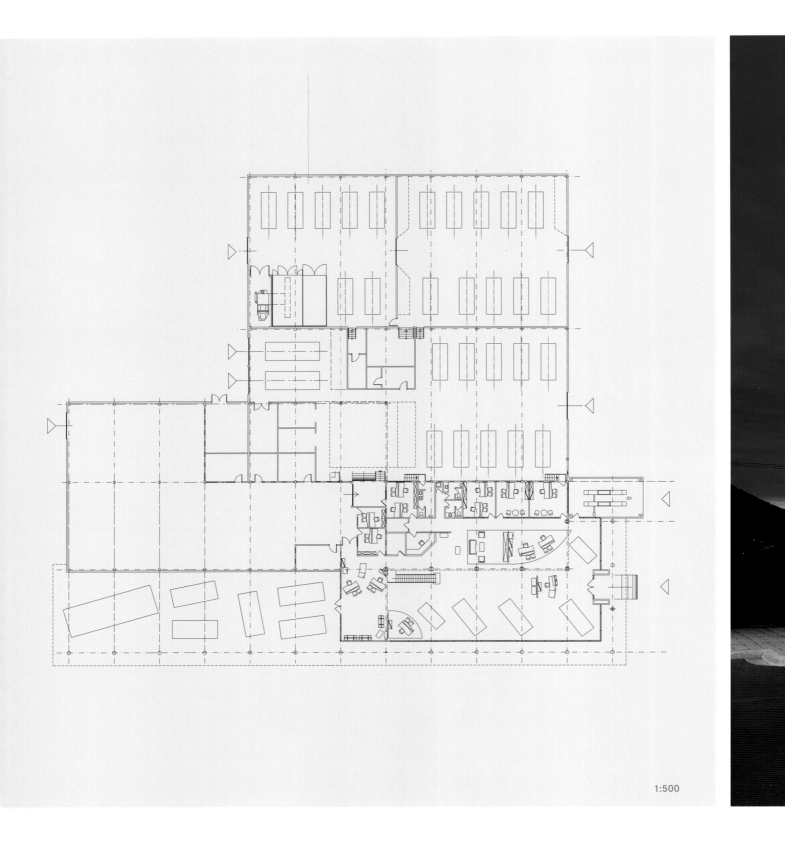

1:500

Ferne Kontinente: Autohäuser in Afrika, Asien und Lateinamerika

Unter dem Vulkan: Mercedes-Benz Autohaus in San Salvador

Under the volcano: Mercedes-Benz showroom in San Salvador

**Innenansichten des Hauses
in San Salvador**

Interior views of the building
in San Salvador

**Freestyle-Architektur in Seoul:
Im relativ chaotischen Stadtbild
der südkoreanischen Metropole
kommt es besonders darauf an,
aufzufallen.**

Freestyle architecture in Seoul:
It is important to be eye-
catching in a relatively chaotic
urban picture of the South
Korean metropolis.

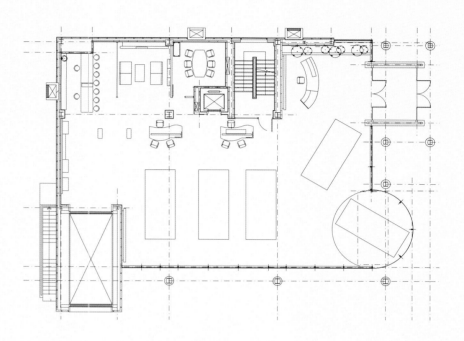

1:250

Ferne Kontinente: Autohäuser in Afrika, Asien und Lateinamerika

**Innenansichten des Auto-
hauses in Seoul**

Interior views of the showroom
in Seoul

Room with a view: Lesbos
Room with a view: Lesbos

Vielleicht die schönste Adresse im Vertriebsnetz von Mercedes-Benz: das Autohaus über der Küste von Lesbos

Perhaps the most beautiful address in the Mercedes-Benz sales network: the showroom above the coast of Lesbos

Room with a view: Lesbos

Die Mercedes-Benz Vertretung auf der griechischen Insel Lesbos repräsentiert derzeit sicher das kleinste, kompakteste Autohausformat der Marke. Positioniert an einem Hang zwischen Wald und Olivenhainen, verfügt das Gebäude mit Meerblick über alles, was ein Autohaus braucht: Showroom, Service, Lager, Büro.

Knapp eine Hand voll Automobile lassen sich im Kundenbereich präsentieren. Platz für raumgreifende Inszenierungen gibt es hier nicht. Eine atmosphärisch dichte Präsentation von Fahrzeugen und Marke ist durch den Ort, das Ambiente, die Insellandschaft und das Küstenpanorama sichergestellt. Auf der Terrassenfläche vor dem Autohaus kann man ohne weiteres Arrangement jene Art von Aufnahmen schießen, mit denen die Werbeindustrie besonders gern den Traum vom Autofahren als vollendetes Freizeitvergnügen darstellt: Im offenen Cabriolet hoch über der Küste das Meer begleiten – geradewegs in einen spektakulären Sonnenuntergang hinein.

Lesbos liegt im Ägäischen Meer dicht vor der Küste Kleinasiens, also der Türkei. Die Insel mit der zerklüfteten Küstenlinie, deren Name sich mit dem der antiken Dichterin Sappho (und deren legendärer Zuneigung zu Frauen) verbindet, ist in der Ausdehnung etwa mit dem Großraum Berlin oder München vergleichbar: Es gibt folglich ein paar plausible Gründe, hier über ein Auto zu verfügen – als Tourist nicht weniger denn als ständiger Bewohner des Eilands. Dabei kommt es den Kunden auf Lesbos in Sachen Technik und Ausstattung wohl weniger auf die Langstreckentauglichkeit eines Fahrzeugs an. Wichtiger ist hier der Fahrkomfort unter den lokalen Straßen- und Klimaverhältnissen.

Sehr selbstverständlich fügt sich das Haus in die Landschaft ein. Dort, wo das Autohaus in den Berg hineingebaut ist, stützen terrassierte Trockenmauern aus Naturstein den Hang, weiter oben tritt der nackte Fels zutage. Das unter der mediterranen Sonne scharf hervortretende, silbrig schimmernde horizontale Lineament der gewellten Metallpaneele des Werkstatt-Trakts kann deshalb an der Rückseite und an den Flanken gemeinsam mit der naturwüchsigen Umgebung interessante Kontraste erzeugen.

Room with a view: Lesbos

The Mercedes-Benz outlet on the Greek island of Lesbos is, at the present time, the smallest, most compact car showroom of the brand. Located on a slope between a forest and olive groves, the building with a sea-view has all the necessary components: showroom, service, warehouse and office.

A very limited number of cars can be displayed in the client area. There is no room for spacious orchestrations. The atmosphere, the island's landscape and the sea panorama make for an ambient and dense brand presentation. On the terrace in front of the building, advertisers like to take photos showing that driving a car can be an accomplished leisure pursuit: driving a cabriolet along the coast into the sunset.

Lesbos is on the Aegean Sea not far from the Turkish coast. The island with the rugged coastline is associated with the name of the antique poet Sappho (and her legendary love of women) and is about as big as the greater urban area of Berlin or Munich. There are a few good reasons for owning a car here – for tourists as well as for locals. For customers on Lesbos long-distance performance of a car is not as important as driving comfort in the local climate and with the local road conditions.

The building is well integrated into the landscape. Where it is built into the mountain, terraced natural stone dry walls support the slope; higher up the naked rock is visible.

When the sun shines on the corrugated metal panels of the workshop, it produces a gleaming silvery effect, which creates an interesting contrast with the natural environment.

Not far from Lesbos, a few islands further on the Aegean Sea, lies the island of Samothrace. In 1863 a big, marble statue of Nike from the second century BC was found. It ended up in France, was exhibited in the Louvre and is now world-famous. It is so famous that the Italian artist Filippo Tommaso Marinetti made it the object of a provocative

Nicht allzu weit von Lesbos, ein paar Inseln weiter in der nördlichen Ägäis, liegt die Insel Samothrake. Hier wurde 1863 eine große, marmorne Nikestatue aus dem zweiten Jahrhundert v.Chr. gefunden. Sie fand ihren Weg nach Frankreich, wurde wegen ihrer klassischen Schönheit an einem prominenten Platz im Pariser Louvre präsentiert und bald weltbekannt. So berühmt, dass der italienische Künstler Filippo Tommaso Marinetti sie zum Gegenstand eines provokanten Vergleichs machte: Die Welt, schrieb Marinetti 1912 im ersten Futuristischen Manifest, sei um eine neue Schönheit reicher geworden – die „Schönheit der Schnelligkeit"; ein schnelles Automobil sei mit seinen schlangengleichen Rohren an der Karosserie „schöner als die *Nike von Samothrake*".

Das war damals, zu Beginn des zwanzigsten Jahrhunderts, eine recht kühne Behauptung. Aus heutiger Sicht ist Marinettis Position, die Werke der bildenden Kunst und technisches bzw. industrielles Design als grundsätzlich ebenbürtige (und damit vergleichbare) Kulturprodukte definierte, durchaus überzeugend. Nirgendwo leuchtet dieser Gedanke schneller ein als in einem Mercedes-Benz Autohaus über der Küste einer griechischen Insel in der Ägäis!

comparison. In 1912 he wrote in his Futuristic Manifesto that the world's wonder had been enriched by a fresh beauty: "the beauty of speed", and that a racing car with its trunk adorned by great exhaust pipes like serpents was "more beautiful than the Victory of Samothrace".

At the beginning of the 20th century, this was a bold statement. For a modern audience Marinetti's position, that works of art and technical or industrial design are fundamentally equal cultural products, seems convincing. Nowhere does this become more apparent than in a Mercedes-Benz showroom above the coast of a Greek island on the Aegean Sea!

**Blick über die Landschaft
aufs Meer**

View of the sea over the
landscape

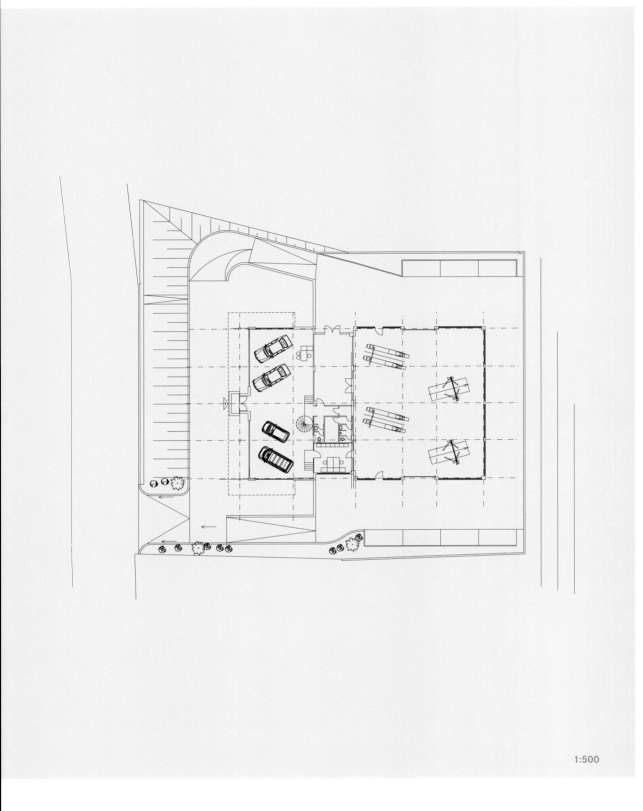

1:500

Auch kleine Terrassen eignen
sich als Markenplattform:
Grundriss des Autohauses
auf Lesbos

Even small terraces are suitable as brand platforms: plan
of the showroom in Lesbos.

Room with a view: Lesbos

Room with a view: Lesbos

Baumhaine und archaisch
anmutende Trockenmauern
prägen das Umfeld des
Autohauses in der Ägäis.

Tree groves and seemingly
archaic dry walls characterise
the surroundings of the
showroom in the Aegean.

Redaktion/Editing	Petra Kiedaisch
	Anja Schrade
Übersetzung/Translation	Vineeta Manglani
Gestaltung/Design	Esther Mildenberger
	www.envisionplus.com
Lithografie/Lithography	Undercover
Produktion/Production	**av**communication GmbH
	Gunther Heeb
Druck/Printed by	Leibfarth + Schwarz GmbH
	+ Co. KG, Dettingen/Erms
Papier/Paper	150g BVS matt

Impressum
Imprint